CAPITOL OF FREEDOM

CAPITOL OF *Freedom*

RESTORING AMERICAN GREATNESS

FIDELIS
BOOKS

KEN BUCK
with SHONDA WERRY

A FIDELIS BOOKS BOOK
An Imprint of Post Hill Press

Capitol of Freedom:
Restoring American Greatness
© 2020 by Ken Buck with Shonda Werry
All Rights Reserved

ISBN: 978-1-64293-507-3
ISBN (eBook): 978-1-64293-508-0

Photographs courtesy of The Architect of the Capitol, Washington, D.C.

Post Hill Press
New York • Nashville
posthillpress.com

Published in the United States of America

This book is dedicated to my favorite freedom fighters:
Bear, Sugar Ray, and Dubya.
The first words uttered by all three of my grandchildren were the same—
"Big government sucks."
May God bless you with a country that promotes a limited
constitutional government, a vibrant civil society with free markets,
strong families, and civic virtue so that you may enjoy opportunity and
freedom. And may God bless the United States.

Contents

Foreword

By Senator Mike Lee

It is a testament to our founders' brilliance that we can still learn from their writings and apply those ideas to today's political problems. I often find myself reaching for my copy of *The Federalist Papers* and other founding documents to help determine the appropriate response to a current problem. "What would James Madison say about this?" is a question I frequently ponder when reviewing legislation. The Founders' wisdom is as applicable today as it was in the eighteenth century.

The Founders remain the authority on matters of the proper scope of government and the relationship between government and individual liberty because they understood human nature. The system of government they devised was a reflection of, rather than a rejection of, human nature. The progressives, by contrast, have gone in the opposite direction. Their social and economic programs all lead to bigger and more intrusive government because of the flawed underlying premise of these proposals. Progressives consistently fail to account for fixed aspects of human life and nature, including, significantly, our desires for more liberty and to be able to provide for our families without government dependence.

As a United States senator, I enjoy the Capitol's many symbols of our founders' political experiment. My desk in the United States Senate Chamber, while appearing similar to other desks, is special to me. The desk, which once belonged to Senator Barry Goldwater—his signature is etched in the wood—serves as a constant reminder to me of the importance of limited government, and the role one individual can play in reversing the trend for ever bigger government.

One of our time-honored traditions in the Senate is selecting our desks. At the start of a new Congress, the desks of departing senators are made available for others. The Senate takes these matters seriously; we even have three Senate resolutions to govern three specific desks and the rules about who may occupy those desks.

When Barry Goldwater's desk became available, I quickly claimed it. I have always felt a strong connection with the former senator and presidential candidate—and not simply because I was born in his home state of Arizona. Goldwater, who almost single-handedly revived conservatism at a time when America desperately needed an alternative to the expansive reach of Big Government, has been an inspiration for my work.

The time Goldwater spent in the Senate, from 1953 to 1965 and then again from 1969 to 1987, coincided with an international craze for far-left politics. Across the globe, Marxist-Leninism was on the rise, gaining a foothold in Asia, Africa, and Latin America. In the United States, conservatism was derided as a backward, anti-intellectual, and entirely unserious political viewpoint. Goldwater changed all of that and helped Americans remember the value of limited government. He was fearless in shaking up the Washington establishment and challenging the status quo.

Goldwater's legacy is intertwined with that of another of my conservative heroes, Ronald Reagan. When Goldwater challenged Lyndon B. Johnson in the presidential race in 1964, a former Democrat and well-known actor named Ronald Reagan embraced Goldwater's brand of conservatism. Reagan's 1964 speech "A Time for Choosing," delivered in October, right before the election, defined America's choice at a pivotal moment. That speech also clearly showcased what conservatism offers—a break from the tyranny of Big Government and, with it, a recommitment to individual liberty.

In the speech, Reagan articulated our political system's unique relationship between the government and the people. "And this idea that government is beholden to the people, that it has no other source of power except the sovereign people, is still the newest and the most unique idea in all the long history of man's relation to man." That simple sentiment neatly sums up the essence of Goldwater's campaign for the White House. In a larger sense, it also perfectly explains what our founders set out to achieve.

Our founders successfully devised a system in which government would be beholden to the people, as Reagan said. But Washington, D.C.'s excessive spending inverts that relationship. Americans today are beholden to, and indebted to, a government that has grown in size and scope, and has become desensitized to the unhealthy relationship between bloated government and the individual.

The challenge for conservatives today is to help make the government, once again, beholden to the people.

I give my constituents tours of the Capitol as often as I am able and I share along the way the founders' vision for the role of government. The Capitol tells that story in a powerful way no textbook quite can.

Along the way during the tour, I highlight two foundational aspects of our system of governance that help ensure the federal government will remain beholden to the people and not the other way around. Our system of federalism empowers the states to hold the federal government in check and thus make it accountable and responsive to the people. Our system of separated powers, and, with it, the system of checks and balances, provides a built-in protection against would-be tyrannical forces within the government. Madison beautifully explained how federalism and separation of powers would complement one another and make government beholden to the people when he wrote in *Federalist 51:* "Hence a double security arises to the rights of the people. The different governments will control each other, and at the same time that each will be controlled by itself."

A favorite spot for me on the tour is the painting in the rotunda, *Washington Resigning His Military Commission.* John Trumbull, who painted this masterpiece, was in London when Washington offered his resignation to the Congress. Even across the ocean, Trumball marveled at the resignation, and remarked that Washington's act simultaneously aroused curiosity and stirred admiration. Individuals, when granted power, so rarely willingly give it up, yet Washington provided a clear case study in good character. Trumbull like our founders, understood power-seeking to be a part of human nature—and something against which to guard.

I share Trumbull's admiration for Washington's conduct and I make a point on the tours of explaining how this singular act symbolizes so many unique features of our government. First, we are reminded of the preeminent role of Congress because his resignation was to the Continental

Congress. Second, Trumbull's use of the empty chair with a cloak draped upon it in the painting is a symbol of a royal throne. Washington in his popularity at the time was regarded almost as royalty. Unlike a king, however, he was stepping down from power and walking away from it. Third, and finally, the painting is a reminder that we have civilian authority over the military—a fact often overlooked, but is vital for protecting individual liberty. Every aspect of Washington's act reminds us that our government is intended to be beholden to the people.

Ken Buck and I first met in 2010 when we ran or the U. S. Senate. As western conservatives, we shared similar values and messages. We both espoused limited government, reduced federal spending, and states' rights. Since Ken arrived in Congress in January 2015, he and I have had many discussions about our responsibility to help restore the right relationship between the individual and the federal government. Our efforts to remind our colleagues of our Article I responsibilities have often fallen on deaf ears, but our resolve remains steadfast. Providing a deeper understanding of the founders' thoughts is the first step in scaling back government. Ken and I view every tour of the Capitol as an opportunity to take in and share the founders' wisdom on the proper scope of government.

This book is an invitation for all Americans to join Ken on a tour, not only of the Capitol building, but also of our heritage of freedom. In the same way *The Federalist Papers* and other founding documents provide insight about the design for our government, the Capitol sheds light on each and every core principle of our government. A deep dive on the features of our liberty experience as Americans is exactly what our nation needs at this critical moment in our history – and it is exactly what Ken delivers here.

Mike Lee
United States Senator from Utah

Introduction

"I know of no way of judging the future but by the past."[1]
—PATRICK HENRY

The bell sounded. It was time for members of the U.S. House of Representatives to cast our vote. Speaker Nancy Pelosi gave her far-left base the red meat they wanted. After months of playing games, the Democrats in the House were moving forward with impeaching President Donald Trump.

Frustrated with the process in the House, I walked with a heavy heart to the most consequential vote of my five years in Congress. With little evidence and even less of a constitutional basis, the impeachment process represented a partisan attack, and set a dangerous opposition strategy for divided government in the future.

On the quick walk from my office to the House floor to vote, I paused a moment in Statuary Hall, my favorite room in the Capitol building. The room once served as the meeting place for the U.S. House of Representatives, back when there were fewer representatives and each member's desk could fit in the grand space. An early example of Greek revival architecture, Statuary Hall is encircled by thirty-eight marble columns. Statues of famous Americans span the perimeter.

As a congressman, I enjoy taking guests on tours of the Capitol. On those tours, I spend most of the time in Statuary Hall because the room has so much to offer, from history to the constitutional lessons.

On this particular December evening, I approached the room with a different feeling. I stared for a few moments at the statue of Lady Liberty

near the ceiling, her hand extended with a scroll. The thirteen-foot statute is perched directly above where the Speaker's desk was previously located in the chamber. I often tell tour guests, "This is one of the most important statues we will see on the tour. She's Liberty, and the scroll in her hand is the Constitution." Ever since 1817, Lady Liberty has offered this remarkable document to members of the House as an eternal reminder of our responsibility to honor the Constitution in everything we do.

Back in the day, it would have been impossible to look at the Speaker's desk without taking in the full glory of Liberty and remembering the Constitution. But not anymore. So much has changed since the House relocated to the current chamber.

Ever since I was first elected to Congress in 2014, I felt an undeniable connection to this particular statue. The first official event in Washington I attended after the election was a dinner in the Capitol for new members of Congress. One of the historians from the Library of Congress joined the dinner to explain the many features of the Capitol. Lady Liberty immediately captured my attention.

The librarian gestured at the magnificent statue. Lady Liberty stood high above us, looking across the room. The American eagle, a symbol of

strength, flanks her on one side, wings flung open. On the other, a serpent snakes up a column, its jaws slightly parted, a manifestation of Sophia, the Greek goddess of wisdom. The librarian didn't need to articulate the meaning of the Constitution in Lady Liberty's outstretched right hand. And the symbolism is unmistakable—wisdom and liberty are intrinsically linked. More specifically, wisdom about our Constitution and the rule of law is the foundation for our liberty.

After drawing everyone's attention to Lady Liberty, the librarian pointed out plaques embedded in the floor where eight former presidents took a seat before or after serving in Congress. John Quincy Adams sat toward the front of the hall. Adams is the only American president to be elected by the House of Representatives because of a tie vote in the electoral college. And yes, that vote of the House occurred in what is now Statuary Hall.

Adams is also the only person to ever win a seat in Congress after serving as president. In the House, we call that career move a promotion.

I often wonder whether Congress should rename Statuary Hall after John Quincy Adams. So much of his life, and even his death, occurred in this hallowed hall. And he had a tremendous impact on America's history. The son of our second president, John Adams, he was a thoughtful and committed leader in the fight to end slavery. In 1836, several members of Congress representing southern states passed a "gag rule," mandating that the House of Representatives automatically table any petition to abolish slavery. Adams fought against that gag rule for a full eight years, before finally helping to repeal it.

When I give tours, guests are always delighted to learn about the special architectural feature in the old House chamber that gave the wily Adams an advantage over his adversaries. The ceiling of the room is designed to resemble ancient Greek meeting places, and its curved shape allows a listener on one side of the room to eavesdrop on a conversation on the opposite side of the room. The architectural feature has such a profound effect that even a whisper can be heard across the room, at the spot where Adams sat. Adams used this feature to his advantage when the pro-slavery Democrats were scheming to silence his abolitionist efforts.

Another famous member of the House had the same passion to abolish slavery. Abraham Lincoln sat at a desk in the back of the chamber from 1847 to 1849, as a congressman from Illinois before he became president. I am often overcome by the thoughts of how past members in this chamber, appropriately called the people's chamber, have tenaciously fought political battles on some of the weightiest topics our nation has ever considered.

Even with my busy travel schedule between Colorado and Washington, I make time to give tours as often as I can because the Capitol has a story to tell, and I want to give voice to that story. I always leave feeling inspired by our founders and our history, and ready to go back and fight the political and policy battles of the day. The Capitol building keeps me grounded in the Constitution and helps me remember our foundational principles.

The Capitol building's lessons are visible and accessible to anyone who will pay attention. However, members of Congress are often too distracted to pay heed to those lessons. I'm familiar with being distracted in the Capitol, and failing to grasp the deeper meaning of the beautiful symbols all around. Back in 1986, I worked as assistant minority counsel for Then Rep. Dick Cheney, before he became vice president. I helped the committee investigating the big political scandal of the day, the Iran-Contra affair, a secret arms deal that came to light during President Reagan's second term. I used to walk through Statuary Hall all the time, but it was simply a room in the Capitol. While working in a cubicle in the windowless fourth floor of the Capitol Dome, I never took the time to learn, to understand, how this remarkable building is a monument to our unique political experiment and our pursuit as a nation to chart a new path with individual liberty as the primary objective.

In addition to Lady Liberty, another statue stands high in Statuary Hall, with an equally important message. Clio, the Greek muse of history, holds a book in which to preserve the events unfolding in the House. She stands ready to record the actions that take place in this legislative body—a reminder to all of us that what Congress does, and how we vote, can have an impact not just today, but for generations to come.

John Quincy Adams was so touched by Clio's poignant reminders that he penned a short poem about the need for members of Congress to be mindful that her book records the actions of Congress. He concludes his poem with: "And let thy volume bear one blessed page / Of deeds devoted to their native land." Performing deeds devoted to our native land. Shouldn't that be the mission statement for every member of Congress?

How many progressive members of Congress passing by Lady Liberty on that fateful night in December 2019, willfully ignored her plea to remember the Constitution? How many of my colleagues asked themselves what John Quincy Adams or Thomas Jefferson would have done in this situation? How many of the progressives who rushed to impeach the president even considered Clio, with her book of remembrance, and what kind of a precedent this unfounded vote would create in the history books?

The impeachment vote illustrates precisely why the lessons of the Capitol are so badly needed today.

On two opposing walls of Statuary Hall, hang artistic copies of the Declaration of Independence. I have often wondered why this founding document is displayed on both sides of the House's meeting spot. I like to think it is displayed on both sides of the aisle as a reminder that this document explains why it was "necessary," in the words of Jefferson, to chart a new path, and to set out on this political experiment. And yet, on this night, my progressive colleagues were ignoring the clear meaning of this document, and were preparing to vote to overturn the will of the people, as expressed in the 2016 election.

Over the past several years, I have made it a point to learn as much as I can about the Capitol, whether as tour guide or as a student. On more than one occasion, my friend and historian David Barton and his son Tim have taken me around the Capitol. I also toured and took notes with the U.S. House historian, the architect of the Capitol, and other professional and amateur historians.

As I have learned along the way, many of my colleagues share my enchantment with this piece of history. I listened a number of times as Congressman Louie Gohmert gave his constituents from Texas a tour, or as Congressman Jody Hice from Georgia led a group of pastors through history. While I am a hands-on learner, I have also sought out books on the history of the Capitol. On my own time, I read material online. On airplanes, shuttling between Washington and Colorado, I took courses on my laptop on American and constitutional history. I quickly learned that much of the literature lacks historical and constitutional context, filling its pages with raw facts and figures about such minutiae as the weight of a statue, the amount of steel tonnage involved in the construction of an edifice, or the number of cracks needed to be repaired somewhere on the dome.

As my piles of research about the Capitol grew, I decided, during my third term in office, it was time to write this book. I want *every* American to understand the meaning behind this magnificent building and its unique architectural features, paintings, inscriptions, and statues. Within these walls, too, are deeply moving stories about our origins as a nation— the American Revolution, concepts important to our founding fathers, their optimism about our country, and this bold experiment in which we are involved.

The Capitol building serves as a monument to our national identity as a free people who charted a new system of self-governance. Even more than that, the building represents the foundational institutions that make America great: Our political institutions, such as our republican form of government, with its elaborate system of checks and balances. And that is strengthened by our social institutions, including the family, the church, and charitable organizations.

To understand where we are, we need to understand where we come from.

The new system of government our founders created after the Revolution was a departure from every prior political arrangement in human history. The intellectual foundation for this uniquely American experiment is rooted in the philosophies of brilliant Europeans of the previous centuries, including John Locke, David Hume, Montesquieu, Jean-Jacques Rousseau, and Voltaire. Whereas European intellectuals debated and discussed the ideas of private property and the moral relationship between the government and the individual, our founders gave life to those radical ideas.

The Declaration of Independence, for one, is steeped in the language of liberty, and echoes the words of Locke. The men who created this new government intended to protect individuals from totalitarian rulers. Individuals did not exist to serve a king or government; instead, the government would serve and protect the individual's interests. The founders understood our rights come from God, not from the government, and are thus "unalienable." Borne out of philosophical debate and political struggle, the founders' vision changed a centuries-old system in which a central authority in the form of a monarch, or emperor, granted the rights of the governed.

The tension between centralized control over the people and individual freedom continues today in the halls of Congress. Every day, in floor debates and committee hearings, I hear progressives giving voice to the failed ideas of totalitarianism, ignoring the revolutionary principles woven into our founding documents.

The truth is, liberals have all but abandoned our Constitution, and so-called conservatives largely ignore the Constitution everywhere but on the campaign trail. But the history of the Capitol doesn't change; it continues to speak the same remarkable story of who we were, who we are, and what we ought to be. It is open for every citizen, every visitor, to ponder how America has lost its way, and even more importantly, how we can get back on track.

"Progressive" is a euphemistic label distorting their true agenda. Our nation's authentic progressives were the founders, who achieved progress by building on the intellectual foundation of the great philosophers. Today's progressives are pushing retrograde and worn-out ideas in favor of more centralized control and less individual autonomy and freedom. Their ideological cousins are the monarchists, Marxists, and fascists. And their tactics are borrowed from those controlling political structures; they advocate for the collective—the group—over the rights of the individual, as a way to take control over our liberties, to circumvent the Constitution.

As part of their agenda, the progressives of today are engaged in a frontal assault on private property rights. For Marxists and progressives, property poses a threat. Private property and private ownership of the modes of production create wealth, and with wealth creation comes income disparity. Marxists and progressives would prefer equal suffering to unequal wealth possession, even if the owner and worker maintain a higher standard of living as a result of the free-market system. The solution to income or wealth disparity, from the progressives' point of view, is to abolish private property.

When we speak of private property today, we often imagine something we can hold or purchase. In a word, we imagine stuff. But for the founders, property was more than physical items. As James Madison articulated, and as the progressives well understand, private property is much broader and expansive than simply our possessions. An individual's right to private ownership includes the right to freedom of speech and freedom of religion.

Private property can also be referred to as an individual's private domain. His thoughts and opinions, his work product, and his writings require the same level of defense and protection from government usurpations as one's private land.

This is where the progressives clash with individual liberty. Each aspect of the private sphere threatens to undermine their agenda of complete control and their emphasis on the collective. An individual's private possessions—which includes his family, his thoughts, his words, his religion, and the physical boundaries of his land—serves as a check on the encroaching federal government. Is it any wonder progressives have systematically attacked the private sphere?

Private property and family life are two of the most important foundations in America, and not coincidentally, they are both intimately connected with individual liberty. Both the family and private property reinforce an individual's existence separate from the government, and create barriers between the individual and the government. In undermining individual property rights in favor of abstractions such as a collective right to property, progressives have simultaneously undermined individual liberty and weakened all aspects of the individual's rights.

Touring the Capitol over a hundred times and contemplating my surroundings, three unique and fascinating features of our founding philosophy stand out for me. First, our nation is a republic, not a democracy, despite the contemporary confusion over what the terms mean and how they are used interchangeably. Many schools no longer require a pledge of allegiance to the flag, but if they honored the practice, it would be a pledge to our flag and the republic for which it stands. As for the definition of *democracy*, imagine rounding up people in a public square and asking them for an impromptu vote, whatever the prevailing sentiment. For the meaning of a *republic*, think about the idea of people electing representatives to make decisions.

The story of our Republic is best described by Benjamin Franklin's exit from the constitutional convention in 1787. Because the convention was held in secret, many citizens gathered outside Independence Hall to learn what type of government the founders crafted. Mrs. Powell asked Benjamin Franklin, as he was leaving the building, "Well, Doctor, what have we got—a monarchy or a republic?" Without hesitation, Benjamin Franklin replied, "A republic, if you can keep it."

Franklin's warning is reflective of the founders' broader recognition that republics require constant vigilance, while democracies, by contrast, inevitably die a predictable death. John Adams conveyed the futility of democracies in a letter to John Taylor. "Remember, democracy never lasts long. It soon wastes, exhausts, and murders itself. There never was a democracy yet that did not commit suicide," he wrote.[2]

Second, in addition to the republican nature of our government, our founders believed a key safeguard to hold the federal government in check within its constitutional scope is the system of separation of powers. Our founders understood pitting the political ambitions of leaders in three different branches of government against each other would protect individual rights. If any branch sought too much power, the other two branches could rein in the overzealous branch.

And third, federalism is a vital feature of our system, a balance between states and the federal government, such that states retain power, with a limited national government, to protect individual liberty and private property rights. Just like the separation of powers, our federalist system is based on respect for our revolutionary form of government, and jealously guarded power among the states with a strong vision of checking a runaway central power. Our founders could never have envisioned what we see today—the federal government silencing state institutions by bribing them with dollars borrowed from China and multinational corporations.

The founders correctly identified each of these three aspects of our system as essential to not just individual liberty, but the longevity of our nation. The genius of our founders is they created a tension between these features based on their understanding of human nature. If any of these balanced features shifted too much in one direction, it would create a weaker form of government.

In the United States today, we find ourselves at a pivotal moment. Benjamin Franklin's words, "if you can keep it," remind us not only of the tenuous nature of this political project our founders established, but also the responsibility we each bear to preserve the institutions vital for our individual liberty. The path we choose will determine our nation's future. The stark contrast is between individual liberty and government control of our lives, often in the name of benefitting the "collective"; it's between preserving our republic, or going down the dangerous and short-lived path of democracy; and it's between respecting the institutions that go hand-in-hand with liberty, like private property, or trampling those vital individual rights. Progressives seek to subordinate our individual rights and liberties for "collective" rights, or for the undefinable "benefit of society."

Another brilliant stroke of our founders is they predicted the nation's future generations would encounter challenges the founders of our nation could not foresee. That's why they crafted the Constitution in such a way to allow for changes through the amendment process. What we see today, especially from progressives, is an impatience to follow the processes for reform. Instead, they want to jettison many features that make our nation great and unique, such as the separation of powers.

Our Constitution is our founders' roadmap for us to chart our future as a free people living in a republic. The Capitol building is the perfect complement to our Constitution. If we just leaned in and paid attention, we would see the Capitol tells the story of our nation's founding, and reminds us of all our cherished constitutionally protected rights and liberties. In my time in Congress, I have come to appreciate that a deep understanding of the Capitol building is as important to understanding our heritage of freedom as is a deep understanding of the Constitution. And it was that realization that sparked my desire to write this book.

In the following pages, I describe our rich history of individual liberty through the lens of the Capitol, highlighting features such as its location, architecture, paintings, and compelling stories that have unfolded in this remarkable building. In examining our founding principles and the values uniting Americans, I delve into modern political discourse—what I have seen and heard during my time in Congress—and compare it to lessons I've experienced every day I have had the honor of serving the people of this great country.

Lady Liberty, extending the Constitution in her hand, reminds all of us—everyday Americans, and lawmakers alike—our success as a nation is rooted in our past and in our founders' brilliant understanding of human nature and the universal desire for freedom.

CHAPTER 1

American Exceptionalism

"We are a nation that has a government—not the other way around.
And this makes us special among the nations of the earth."[1]

—RONALD REAGAN

The echoes of the past, reverberating in Statuary Hall, often inspire a discussion among the tourists about our unique history. Whether it is the dark stain of slavery and how we fought among ourselves to right that moral catastrophe, or our focus on the western wilderness and manifest destiny, there is plenty of evidence of American exceptionalism in the Capitol. We just need to look.

"Does anybody know why our capital is located in Washington, D.C.?"

It's a straightforward question, and one I invariably ask when I start my tours. The answer is also unknown to most of those who join me on this excursion into our storied past.

In groups of fifteen to twenty people, silence tends to prevail. A middle school child, up to speed on her civic class reading, might note some obscure knowledge, including how the capital was once in New York.

But why D.C.?

Most people are flummoxed, and for good reason.

The unlikely Washington backstory sets the stage for America's unfolding story of exceptionalism.

President George Washington took office in 1788, in New York City, the first capital city. By the time he was re-elected in 1792, the capital had already moved to Philadelphia. Congress subsequently approved the Residence Act, calling for the creation of a free-standing national capital, with the intent to move it from Philadelphia. It remained in Philadelphia for ten years, until growing controversy brought its location once again to congressional attention. President Washington, by the way, holds the distinction of being the only president to be sworn into office in two capital cities.

The founders understood if this American experiment in self-governance was to succeed, it needed a place where representatives from every state could come together and speak for the people—not housed in a state or state capital, but in its own place. Finding the right location and the infrastructure for a capital city was a challenge the founders set out to address quickly.

European countries established centers of power around pre-existing, well-established cities. London became the capital of England in the 12th century, mainly for its large population and established role as a trade hub. Paris existed long before France united as a country. It already possessed deep cultural and political roots.

The founders sought instead to create a new system of government, and the notion of a capital city for the new nation housed in a state undermined the idea of preserving states' voices. By way of contrast, they wanted to make it clear the creation of a capital city was to be a distinct nod to the invention of a government not by "accident" or "force," but resulting from "reflection and choice," as Alexander Hamilton aptly put it, in *Federalist* No. 1.[2] The founders believed they could establish good government by the people and for the people—but only with purposeful planning and a fearless sense of self-awareness. Thus, they chose the location we now know as Washington, D.C., to be the site of the capital for this new experiment in freedom.

The decision was a compromise, symbolic of the American political process. Despite their differences, the thirteen colonies gathered in the name of inalienable rights. Whether you hailed from a South Carolina farm or Massachusetts metropolis mattered little. What was important was this capital district belonged to no single faction, party, or state, but was stewarded by all.

The location of the capital set the tone for the country's direction. Consequently, statesmen with even the noblest intentions were eager to lure it their way. For example, Thomas Jefferson of Virginia, and those representing other southern states, wanted the capital district in a location more supportive of agriculture. Meanwhile, Hamilton, whose main priority was for the newly created federal government to assume the debts accumulated during the Revolutionary War, wanted the capital closer to the financial centers of the country, then in Philadelphia. Out of thirty-two other sites considered, the land between Virginia and Maryland on the Potomac River appeased both sides, in part because it represented a balance between north and south and slave and non-slave states. Notable as well, the fight over the placement of the capital turned into the first large-scale lobbying campaign our country knew.

The decision to move the capital to Washington, D.C., showcased not only the importance of compromise in American politics, but also the importance of federalism. Federalism was the founders' idea that our sovereign states would be united into one sovereign nation. A federal government would unify the states, but not subjugate them. Thus, it was no accident the nation's capital was moved to a non-state. The Articles of Confederation, the first Constitution of the thirteen original states, badly needed reform, lacking a strong central government. Our United States Constitution attempted to address that problem, outlining how these states would work together but retain a level of self-governance.

Establishing the capital within an existing state would have left the door open for political favoritism for that state, and for potential conflicts of interests between the state and federal governments. Another option, to give the capital its own statehood, led to the same dead end, raising the same issues. Thus, these men decided Washington, D.C., would be a federal district only, ensuring no one state would have more power or leverage in the federal government.

How important was it to the founders? They even wrote the parameters of location into the new Constitution. James Madison outlined the reasoning behind this provision, in *Federalist* No. 43, calling the arrangement an "indispensable necessity."

"The indispensable necessity of complete authority at the seat of government carries its own evidence with it…. Without it, not only the public authority might be insulted and its proceedings interrupted with impunity; but a dependence of the members of the general government on the State comprehending the seat of the government, for protection in the exercise of their duty, might bring on the national councils an imputation of awe or influence, equally dishonorable to the government and dissatisfactory to the other members of the Confederacy."[3]

French architect Pierre Charles L'Enfant, a friend of George Washington, who served valiantly on the side of the rebellious colonials, was tapped to design the new capital. When he surveyed the land that would one day become the national capital, he recognized an opportunity. He strategized an effective yet symbolic city, drawn from a plan "wholly new."[4] Using the area's natural topography, he designed the city with equality specifically in mind. The Capitol building, the house of the people, would sit at the center of the city and on the highest point, rather than the president's residence, as would have been befitting in a European monarchy setting. The streets would be wide, organized, and with a nod to the states' important role in the republic, the diagonal streets would be named after each state, such as we see today: Massachusetts, Vermont, New Hampshire, et al.

No doubt European powers laughed at the sight of freedom's exceptional new home. The land ceded by Virginia and Maryland to host the nation's political hub was swampy farm land. As strange as it may seem,

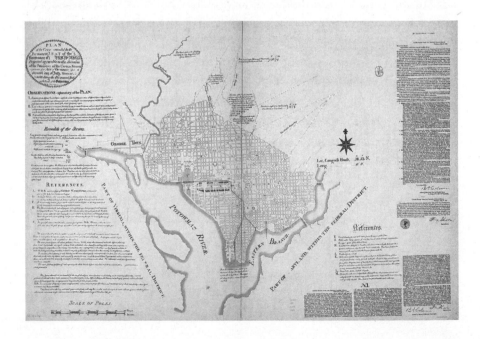

this site said something profound about the new nation. Ours would be one purposefully shaped from wild land. It would not come easily, and would require ongoing effort to maintain.

An Exceptional View of Government

A pressing question on everyone's mind at the time was, *Could people really govern themselves?* The founders set out with an ambitious goal—to create a relationship between the federal government and individuals, as never seen before. Under this new system, the government derived its authority from the consent of the governed, creating a built-in system of account-ability and limited government.

That extraordinary relationship between the government and individual is reflected in one of the most exceptional features of American government—our right to petition our government. And the city plan reflects that freedom we have as Americans. L'Enfant made sure to include an open mall area where any and all citizens could come together in front of their representative leadership to peacefully assemble and petition the government. The Mall, which today is taken for granted as part of the landscape in our nation's capital—a place for picnics and the like—has served a functional and symbolic purpose in our history of freedom.

The right to petition the government is protected in the First Amendment, although it is often overlooked because of the attention we give to the other enumerated freedoms, including the freedom of the press, freedom of speech, and freedom of religion. The founders were serious about creating an accessible and approachable government. Their experience with the unresponsive British crown fueled that concern. We can still hear the founders' impatience with unresponsive government. Thomas Jefferson wrote, in the Declaration of Independence, about the Americans' experience with the royal government. "In every stage of these Oppressions We have Petitioned for Redress in the most humble terms: Our repeated Petitions have been answered only by repeated injury. A Prince whose character is thus marked by every act which may define a Tyrant, is unfit to be the ruler of a free people."

Edmund Burke, a member of the House of Commons of Great Britain during the Revolutionary War, commented on the intellectual advantage

17

the Americans had in this debate with the British king about the oppressions they were facing. In a speech in 1775, Burke remarked, "For, in order to prove that the Americans have no right to their liberties, we are every day endeavoring to subvert the maxims which preserve the whole spirit of our own. To prove that the Americans ought not to be free, we are obliged to depreciate the value of freedom itself."[5]

The founders wanted to devise a new form of responsive and attentive government, and the Mall and accessible Capitol building were two parts of the plan. To this day, people still gather in that wide-open space, to learn, to explore, to fellowship, to challenge, and even to protest. The March for Life, and other important expressions of petitioning the government, take place on this honored strip of land.

Perhaps less well known is the story of L'Enfant's firing as city planner in 1792, a stark action showing precisely why the founders wanted a limited role for the government. But what exactly precipitated Washington's decision to fire his old comrade? The story is an important part of our heritage as free people.

In building the new city, L'Enfant encountered an obstacle for one of his new roads—the private home of Daniel Carroll, a prominent landowner in the area. Not to be deterred from his city designs, L'Enfant had the home demolished, paying little attention to Mr. Carroll's property rights or the purpose for which the new federal government existed—namely, *to protect* individual liberty.

President Washington was distressed to learn about the seizure and destruction of private property, and consulted with Thomas Jefferson, who in turn, consulted with James Madison about the issue. Jefferson drafted the letter for the president to send to L'Enfant, and President Washington also wrote a letter to Daniel Carroll to apologize for the city planner's "zeal."[6]

Stop and think about the significance of that episode in history. The president of the United States consulted with other founders of our great nation to determine the correct course of action because one private citizen's property rights were violated. Our founders knew this new system required the government to respect individuals' rights. There simply was no way to overlook an instance of trampling basic property rights.

An Exceptional Problem-Solving Ability

Here's an example of one of our nation's defining features: The federal government didn't seize land from Maryland and Virginia to create a capital city. The two states simply agreed to cede the land of their own volition.

I like to point this out during my Capitol tours because it illustrates, in real terms, our ability to solve our problems without abandoning our identity of freedom or rejecting the Constitution.

President Ronald Reagan, perhaps more than any other president, exemplified the attitude that our nation is exceptional and how we can tackle problems by remaining true to our constitutional principles. In the rotunda, the statue of Reagan—vibrant in bronze hues—is another favorite spot on the tour. President Reagan's can-do attitude is still a source of inspiration for Americans.

On a recent tour, a man wandered from the group to stand next to the Reagan statue. While touching the base of the statue, he asked if it was true the base contains a portion of the Berlin Wall, a vestige of the Cold War that once divided East and West Germany, communism from capitalism. I assured him what he read is true; the base includes pieces of concrete from the Berlin Wall, where President Reagan gave his famous speech, with the freedom-reverberating line challenging the Soviet leader, "Mr. Gorbachev, tear down this wall!"[7]

Reagan's optimism about America's future is memorialized on the statue, emblazoned with the words of the 1992 speech he delivered at the Republican National Convention in Houston: "America's best days are yet to come. Our proudest moments are yet to be. Our most glorious achievements are just ahead."[8] That optimism flowed from Reagan's understanding that we have the tools we need to solve any challenge confronting our nation. Our Constitution, our spirit of innovation, and our commitment to individual liberty were the sources of his outlook on America's future.

Contrast Reagan's sense of our strength as a nation with what we see today. Progressives bemoan problems we encounter as a reason to jettison the Constitution, or even worse, adopt failed European socialist policies, denigrating individual rights in the name of the collective. American exceptionalism is no longer a key feature helping to drive our problem-solving; instead, progressives look for ways to put into place bloated government policies to solve all our problems. Here, of course, Reagan's wisdom serves as a check on the liberals' plans. He famously said, "…[G]overnment is not the solution to our problems; government is the problem."[9]

As the Left ramps up its plans to trade in American exceptionalism for even bigger government, there has never been a more critical time for us to listen to the Capitol's message of freedom. The national conversation about socialism necessitates a countrywide discussion about American exceptionalism rooted in property rights, individual liberty, and freedom from the control of government. Socialism's history is a story of tyranny, oppression, limited options, and the stifling expansion of the relationship between the government and individual. The normalization of socialism leads us further away from our founding principles into not just unwise, but dangerous territory.

The Clash over American Exceptionalism

The message of American exceptionalism, on display everywhere in the Capitol, is at odds with the message we are barraged with in the media, in our schools, and from many liberal politicians. Take, for example, when former President Barack Obama dismissed American exceptionalism, stating: "I believe in American exceptionalism, just as I suspect that the Brits believe in British exceptionalism, and the Greeks believe in Greek exceptionalism."[10] Obama's insistence on equating American exceptionalism with British or Greek views of their own exceptionalism highlights how little he understands about the defining aspects of our unique role in the political project, and in charting individual liberty.

It has become politically correct to cast doubt on America's exceptionalism, and increasingly popular to attack the notion outright. We see the basic questioning of America all over the media. We hear it in the steady stream of liberal extremism spouted by Congresswoman Alexandria

Ocasio-Cortez, including her nonsensical claim, "Right now we have this no-holds-barred, Wild West hyper-capitalism. What that means is profit at any cost. Capitalism has not always existed in the world, and it will not always exist in the world."[11] I am constantly amazed how often I hear my colleagues in Congress downplaying American exceptionalism, whether they are questioning our role in being a voice of freedom for other nations, or praising the un-American socialist system.

When I give tours of the Capitol, however, I can always sense from the guests they understand the exceptional nature of America. I wrongly attributed this insight to my guests' tendency to be conservatives from Colorado, who must somehow be smarter than other Americans. As I took tours with my congressional colleagues, I learned their constituents were equally perceptive. Now I believe Americans recognize the messages emanating from the Capitol better than many of the people who work in this building. At least our tourists refuse to ignore the obvious, while our elected officials have to ignore that which violently conflicts with their policy proposals.

I see the stark contrast daily, at the Capitol. I see American exceptionalism throughout the Capitol—from our founding to our spirit of innovation to our system of checks and balances. Then I listen in amazement to the message of my liberal colleagues. They aren't merely dismissive of American exceptionalism; they are often openly hostile to the idea and they are willing to do whatever it takes to dismantle the features of our country that make us exceptional. When liberals in Congress talk about implementing socialism, packing the Supreme Court, doing away with the Electoral College, taking away our Second Amendment rights, or their many attempts to do away with the First Amendment's protections of free speech and freedom of religion, they are demonstrating just how little value they place on American exceptionalism.

The Threat of Socialism

A man walks into a shop in the Soviet Union. He asks the clerk, "You don't happen to have any bread, do you?" The clerk says, "No, we're the fish store. We don't happen to have any fish. You're looking for the bread store across the street. They don't happen to have any bread."

You might know the joke. Except it isn't really funny if you think about the consequences of what it suggests about socialism, an economic system under which the state owns the modes of production, and private individuals are not vested in the profit-making structures of businesses. But it would be wrong to think of socialism as *only* an economic system. Socialism is an all-encompassing government system. What starts out as a utopic economic idea, quickly takes over all aspects of society. That's why it is so alarming liberals today are embracing socialism as a feel-good alternative to capitalism.

When we think about the exceptional features of our government, it is impossible to separate our prosperity as a nation from our free-market capitalist identity. And yet that's exactly what liberals today are attempting to do.

The aforementioned Ocasio-Cortez, who in her first term in Congress has already announced herself as capitalism's major foe, said during a speech in Austin, Texas, "Capitalism is irredeemable." The statement shows how misguided she is about America's heritage, and reflects her deeply flawed understanding of the economic forces undergirding our liberty.

Socialism asserts individuals should not be able to keep the profits of their own labor. In this regard, socialism fails to understand one of the most fundamental characteristics of human nature—we are motivated by being rewarded for our work. The desire to make a living, to improve our situation in life, and to provide for our children are ingrained in human nature. But socialism denies each of those desires and pretends those human desires are evil and corrupting.

President Obama was one who failed to understand the free market, or the incentive structures motivating people to work so hard to create wealth—not only for themselves, but also for others. In a 2010 speech in Illinois, Obama said, "I do think at a certain point you've made enough money."[12] Implicit in this statement was Obama's unstated call to action, that there should be a redistribution system in place to ensure people who have "made enough money" are contributing the "excess" money, as determined by the government, back to the collective. But is he willing to put his money where his mouth is and share all the money he's made from his bestselling books?

Obama's radical views on labor and profits were also on display when he made the famous remark, in a 2012 campaign speech in Roanoke, Virginia, "If you've got a business—you didn't build that."[13] The statement was news, of course, to the millions of hardworking business owners in America who know they did build their businesses. It would be a mistake for us today to view Obama's statement that business owners and job creators did not build their own businesses, as simply a clumsy gaffe on the campaign trail. Instead, it represents an important first step in creating class warfare—or as Marx would say, "class consciousness." Obama was a student of Marxist theory and no doubt aware the American public would only buy into socialist policies once there was widespread discontent about business owners' profits.

More than two hundred years before Barack Obama became president, another president, Thomas Jefferson, warned about wealth redistribution and government confiscation of individuals' profits. In his first inaugural address in 1801—he was the first president to take the oath in the new capital of Washington, D.C.—Jefferson described what good government looks like. "A wise and frugal government…shall restrain men from injuring one another, shall leave them otherwise free to regulate their own pursuits of industry and improvement, and shall not take from the mouth of labor the bread it has earned. This is the sum of good government."

Like Jefferson, James Madison was another founding father who thought deeply about the relationship between property and freedom. In his 1792 "Essay on Property," he explained government's chief purpose is to protect property. "Government is instituted to protect property of every sort; as well that which lies in the various rights of individuals, as that which the term particularly expresses. This being the end of government, that alone is a just government which impartially secures to every man whatever is his own."[14]

The idea that government should not interfere with individuals' economic pursuits or take away the fruits of their hard work is a fundamental and cherished feature of America's success story. It's difficult to think of an idea that fails to comprehend the reason for America's success, or would surely fritter away our prosperity more than socialism. And yet liberals today want to move to socialism.

The founders' statements about capitalism, private enterprise, and the defense of private property are backed up by their actions. The story about L'Enfant's dismissal as city planner shows that, for the founders, private property was more than a good idea; the defense of private property was to be the foundation for our new country, and would be one of the defining concepts of our exceptionalism.

American exceptionalism was the topic of Alexis de Tocqueville's book, *Democracy in America,* which was published in two volumes, in 1835 and 1840, after a substantial undertaking by the Frenchman to study America's unique political and social structures. His book provides an outsider's appreciation of everything making America unique and exceptional. Those characteristics de Tocqueville identified are as important today as they were nearly two hundred years ago, if we hope to retain our exceptional nature.

De Tocqueville identified many exceptional aspects of life in America that directly contribute to our unique political system, including our religious beliefs, our emphasis on family, our local government and associations, and our can-do attitude, which compels us to tackle political and social problems through charity and local solutions. Those unique and exceptional features of American life are still part of who we are as Americans today, but if we aren't careful, they will diminish as politicians seek to dismantle each of those core ideas of our identity.

When we look at the beautiful, wide-open Mall, we see a place for the people to petition their government. We see the Lincoln Memorial and are reminded of the president's courage in the face of the dark stain of slavery. Wherever we look—in the heart of a capital district carved out of a swamp—we are reminded of our exceptionalism, an experiment in self-governance resulting in the creation of prosperity far exceeding what any other country in the history of the world has ever witnessed. We, as a nation, are proud of our diversity, of working with the same Constitution we began with, and of our greatness. That's why I tell the story of American exceptionalism, on Capitol tours. It's also why I always ask myself, *Can we expect future generations of Americans to protect and preserve America's exceptional greatness if they don't even understand it?*

To modify Benjamin Franklin's warning—we have an *exceptional* republic, if we can keep it. And our ability to keep it is tied to our understanding and appreciation of our exceptionalism.

CHAPTER 2

A Pedestal Waiting for a Monument

"In republican government, the legislative authority
necessarily predominates."[1]

—JAMES MADISON

The crypt of the U.S. Capitol isn't the dark, dank dwelling conjured up by its evocative moniker.

On the contrary, the crypt is a well-lit circular chamber on the ground floor, under the rotunda, traversed by countless people every day, hurrying on their way—blinders on—to a hearing or meeting of reputed import.

George Washington was supposed to be interred here—hence the name of the burial place—but his body never made it. Construction of the crypt was interrupted by the War of 1812. His family decided to honor his wish to be buried at his Mt. Vernon, Virginia home, just a few miles away from the Capitol.

Tucked away in the crypt—hidden in plain sight—is a replica of the Magna Carta, the eight-hundred-year-old document reining in the monarch. On tours, I make a point of directing my visitors' attention to this transformational declaration; otherwise, they might miss it, given all the magnificent distractions surrounding it—forty neoclassical columns, and thirteen statues of prominent Americans of the original thirteen colonies.

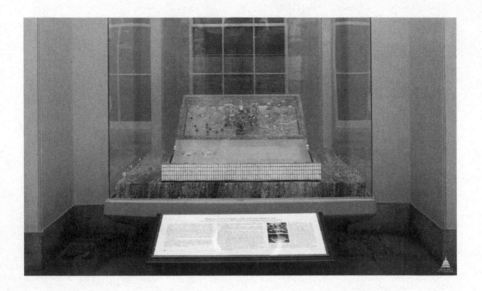

In all the times I've entered the crypt—and it's been plenty—I've never seen people clustered around the gold and glass case containing this most essential document, the greatest relic in the room.

The history of the Magna Carta predates our nation's founding by more than five hundred fifty years, which might explain how it sometimes escapes people's attention today. King John of England signed the Magna Carta on June 15 of 1215, after a severe clash with his barons, who had become frustrated with the monarch's arbitrary rule and abuses of power. The noblemen set out to craft a document to rein in the king's powers. The document they formulated prohibited arbitrary arrest and imprisonment, and established individuals' right to a fair trial and the protection of private property. Those rights are foundational to the rule of law, and essential for limiting the powers of government.

The Magna Carta—Latin for *the Great Charter*—provided the key principles of the supremacy of the rule of law which formed the foundation of our Constitution. In this respect, it is symbolic that the Magna Carta replica lies in the crypt—the literal foundation—of the Capitol, erected to support the rotunda above it. The document's most important principle—that no man is above the law, not even the king—is the foundation for American rule of law, and the base upon which we have built our system of government.

If those basic rights recognized in the Magna Carta sound familiar, it's for good reason. America's founders drew heavily from the ideas in the Magna Carta to write the American Declaration of Independence and the Constitution.

Only a few feet away from the Magna Carta is a worn white marble stone compass star embedded in the center of the floor of the crypt. While it may seem, at first glance, the two features of the Capitol are unrelated, they each reinforce the primacy of the rule of law and the importance of the legislative body.

That compass star is the point in Washington, D.C. where all four quadrants of the district—northeast, southeast, northwest, and southwest—converge. If you place your foot on the compass, as I have from time to time to demonstrate for my visitors, you are standing in all four quadrants of the city simultaneously. When I take tourists to this spot, the following ritual tends to take place: They stand on the star, which droops below floor level, smoothed down with the passage of time. Then they hop off the star, pull out their smartphones, and take photos of what is, admittedly, a cool symbol. But it holds even greater significance. The compass star is the key to understanding the vital role the legislature plays in our republic.

* * *

We must first revisit Pierre-Charles L'Enfant.

After he wrote to President George Washington, offering to create a capital "magnificent enough to grace a great nation,"[2] he got the gig in 1791. Influenced by the France of his youth, L'Enfant borrowed ideas from the grand sweep of the Versailles palace, conjuring up what are now distinct D.C. features, such as its broad avenues, designed on a slashing angle. The cheerful L'Enfant sought another epic brush stroke, designing a considerable park in front of the White House, for the benefit of the president, whoever happened to be in residence. But Thomas Jefferson put the kibosh on those plans out of a worry such an exclusive domain didn't mesh with the nascent nation of the people. Hence, the space became a public gathering spot you might have heard of—Lafayette Park.

L'Enfant, though, got his way on a more vital part of his plan, to make the Capitol the central point of the new capital district. The Capitol was created to be the central focus of the new government, a building perched on a slight hill, elevated above the rest of the city. That hill was known in our nation's earlier years as "Jenkins Hill," because a man named Thomas Jenkins apparently once grazed livestock at the site. L'Enfant saw it in a more enchanted way, as "a pedestal waiting for a monument."[3] That pedestal has come to be known as Capitol Hill, today.

The location of the Capitol building speaks volumes about the role our founders intended the legislative branch to play—and the paramount role of the rule of law. Because the Capitol is located on a hill, on one of the highest points in Washington, D.C., it reminds all of us that the legislative branch—the part of the federal government most accountable to the people—is the most important branch of government.

The Three Unequal Branches

We often hear the federal government has three "co-equal" branches. That long-held idea is often taught in school. Heck, many of my own colleagues in Congress parrot this notion. Some go so far as to abdicate their constitutional role for a simple but unenviable reason: they don't want to make the tough decisions. Members of Congress, after all, are beholden to a two-year election cycle, and unfortunately, some bow to short-term political realities over the long-term needs of our country. But this, of course, isn't what our founders intended. They didn't envision equal branches. James Madison made that clear when he said, "In republican government, the legislative authority necessarily predominates."[4]

The legislature, to be sure, was intended to hold the most important role in government. In its specified powers and oversight responsibilities of the other two branches, we are able to glean the founders' view of how important the legislature would be.

It is worth noting the legislature was front and center on the minds of our founders, and they appropriately placed the overview of this branch in the first article of the Constitution. Why were the founders so determined to make the legislative branch the preeminent aspect of the federal government? In large part, this desire was the result of their odious experience with the British crown. The founders were clear about their struggles with the British king. As Jefferson wrote in the Declaration of Independence, their experience with the king of Great Britain was a "history of repeated injuries and usurpations," all leading to the establishment of an "absolute tyranny."

As Jefferson went on to explain, the British king refused to provide his assent to laws, even those most "necessary for the public good." He called together legislative bodies at places "unusual, uncomfortable, and distant from the Public Records," which Jefferson believed was the king's attempt to fatigue the legislators "into compliance with his measures." Further, the king dissolved representative houses that stood up to him about his repeated "invasions on the rights of the people."

Notice the pattern in each of those grievances. The first of the injuries Jefferson listed was about the relationship between the king and legislature. The founders saw that a weak legislature, lacking the power to hold the king in check, led to a tyrannical regime.

The Declaration of Independence further enumerates other grievances caused by the too-powerful king, including his decision to make judges dependent on him for their salaries and tenures, the standing armies he kept without the consent of the legislators, and the taxes he imposed without the consent of the governed.

With these tyrannies in mind, the founders of our new nation set out to accomplish two related goals: First, to ensure the legislative body would be appropriately empowered to guard against the president's acquisitive desire for more power; and second, to hold the executive in check by making it clear his authority is dependent upon, and in response to, the legislature.

When you read our Constitution and the Declaration of Independence together, you can see a clear thought pattern from our founders. Wanting to avoid the tyranny of a monarch, they gave the legislature the power to write laws, provide consent to the president's appointments (the Senate's role), approve judicial nominees (again, in the Senate), impeach officers of the executive and judicial branches, determine how federal funding is spent (the "power of the purse"), and the important power to declare war.

In addition to the weighty authorities residing within the legislature, we can also understand the founders' intention for the legislature to be the most important branch of government because of its relationship to the other two branches. The legislature, as we have seen, exists to make the laws. The executive branch exists to enforce those laws created by the legislative branch, and the judicial branch exists to offer opinions when clashes arise from different interpretations of those laws. In each case, however, the legislature's role—writing the laws—is a necessary precursor for the functions of the executive and judicial branches.

Again, it is worth noting James Madison's observation that the legislative body is supreme. That's because we are a republic rooted in the rule of law. If we were a pure democracy, the laws would be subordinated to the fluctuating will of the majority. And if we were a monarchy, as disdainful to the founders as was Great Britain's, the laws would be the product of one man's whims.

The People's Capitol

Imagine a society without the rule of law.

Hard to do, right?

That's because we take for granted how we live in a society where the rule of law prevails.

Not only could our founders imagine such a capricious world without the rule of law, they lived through it, under the weight of the British monarch. The founders, who studied the European political philosophers, understood in order for the rule of law to play a paramount role in society, the people would need to give their consent to the framework of the rule of law. Additionally, the rule of law would need to reflect the will of society, not the whims of a single ruler or king.

To protect against the vacillating desires of one ruler, or even of one king from day to day, the power to make laws rests with Congress, the legislative branch. The legislative branch is an expression of the people's will, as the members who serve in Congress are there because they were elected by the people. Even before the Seventeenth Amendment allowed for the direct election of United States senators, the Senate was accountable to the states, which, in turn were held accountable by the people. Congress is to be a responsive body, in tune with the American people.

One way to ensure Congress remains in touch with Americans is to make sure the legislature's office buildings—the Capitol and the Capitol complex—are open to the public. If you have toured the Capitol and the White House, you have probably noticed a few differences. For starters, you cannot simply show up at the White House door and walk in. You must be on a pre-screened list, or you must secure tour tickets in advance. To be placed on the pre-screened list for a meeting, you must provide your social security number for a background check, and then your name will be placed on the visitor list for the day.

By contrast, the Capitol and Capitol complex buildings, including all the House and Senate office buildings, remain open to the public, and that is helpful to preserving our republican form of government.

On any given weekday, whether Congress is in session or not, when you walk the halls of the House or Senate office buildings, you will encounter thousands of Americans coming to Congress for meetings with staff members, to educate members of Congress, and to advocate for certain policies. That cherished First Amendment right to petition the government is on display every day.

In the Cox Corridors on the first floor of the Capitol's House wing, a famous quote is inscribed on one of the walls—courtesy of Alexander Hamilton—serving as a reminder for members of Congress: "Here, sir, the people govern."[5]

I am always inspired and humbled by those five simple words, which are the heart of our constitutionally limited government, and the essence of our republican form of government.

When American citizens come to the Capitol, or when they meet with a member of Congress, or send an email or letter to a member's office, they are engaging in the political process and serving as an accountability partner with Congress. We are sometimes stopped—though, certainly not always—in our tracks from passing bad bills, because American citizens are willing to do the hard work required by our republic, of reading bill language, engaging in conversations with members of Congress about how to improve the bills, and even reminding members of Congress and congressional staff about the Constitution's guidance for us.

I have had the opportunity to sit in my office in the Rayburn House Office Building and visit with constituents about the merits or flaws of legislation, and I am always impressed with their knowledge, not only of the bill text, but of the Constitution. I'm reminded of meetings with students and faculty from Colorado Christian University, for instance. They always come well-prepared, having studied the issue, such as religious freedom. The depth of their questions can even reach the rarified level of trying to understand the unintended, nuanced consequences of a U.S. Supreme Court decision about, say, same-sex marriage, and the impact on married student housing at a private religious university.

Meetings with such savvy constituents help me carry out the function I was elected to perform—to serve as a lawmaker representing the people of the 4th Congressional District of Colorado, and to ensure our nation continues to respect the rule of law.

In a republic, citizens are expected to engage in political accountability. The system falls apart without the watchful eye of the voters. Coming to Congress and writing to Congress are a big part of providing accountability. Another key part of accountability, of course, is the election system. James Madison, in Federalist No. 39, explains the importance of elections, by saying, "We may define a republic to be…a government which derives all its powers directly or indirectly from the great body of the people, and is administered by persons holding their offices during pleasure for a limited period, or during good behavior."[6] In times of poor behavior, it goes without saying voters will kick the misbehaving member out of office at election time.

Our founders carefully devised different election methods for the House and the Senate. All 435 House members are elected for only a two-year term, and they are elected by the people they will represent in Congress. The Senate, by contrast, is comprised of a hundred members who are each elected to serve a six-year term. Originally, senators were chosen by their state legislatures, but the Seventeenth Amendment to our Constitution changed that. Many conservatives believe that was a mistake. Senators sent to the Senate by their legislature were held to a higher level of accountability to the concerns of their home states.

Modern Assaults on the Rule of Law

Here's one thing that doesn't come up on my Capitol tours: the delicate balance between the rule of law and liberty.

We don't want a country so laden with laws it becomes oppressive. At the same time, we don't want to ignore the rule of law and let people do whatever they want, for the obvious reason we would have nothing but chaos. A dense subject for a tour, perhaps. James Wilson articulated the importance of the counterbalance, in a series of law lectures given at the College of Philadelphia, from 1790–1792, entitled *Of the Study of the Law in the United States*. He wrote: "Without liberty, law loses its nature and its name, and becomes oppression. Without law, liberty also loses its nature and its name, and becomes licentiousness."[7] Put another way: Liberty in this country can only exist because we have the rule of law. Likewise, the rule of law only exists as we know it because we have individual liberty.

First, laws must be consistent with the Constitution and our framework of individual liberty. Second, laws must be equally and consistently applied, even to the powerful people who hold positions in government. Third, laws must be easily understandable by the public. What good is it, after all, if the laws are so complex that average citizens are unable to understand them? Finally, laws must be crafted by the legislature, the branch of government accountable and responsive to the public.

In recent years, as the federal government has grown, it has overtaken the governing of our day-to-day lives in a way unimaginable to our founders. Hand in hand with this rapid expansion of government, Congress has increasingly passed off its lawmaking authorities to executive agencies, creating a massive and unaccountable administrative state.

We can also think about it this way: If Congress crafts a bill that will have a negative effect on your family or business, you can schedule a meeting with your representative in the House or your two senators. You can exercise your First Amendment right to petition the government. But what happens if that new proposed law is being considered by an executive agency? Where would you even begin to start the petitioning process? Bureaucrats in the labyrinth of Washington, D.C.'s administrative state are unaccountable to voters, as they are not elected to their positions, and are, thus, unresponsive to the needs of the American people.

As Congress has gotten into the habit of handing off its constitutionally specified duties to unaccountable agencies within the executive branch, the lawmaking process has become even more distant from the American people. This trend is dangerous for our republic.

The Investigative Power

One of the most significant Congressional functions is absent from any mention in the Constitution. It relates to the supremacy of the legislative branch's rule of law. The power of Congress to investigate and provide oversight is implied in the Constitution, but not clearly spelled out. The Constitution grants Congress "all legislative powers," and the Supreme Court, over the years, has concluded the investigative authority is one the founders intended to give Congress.

One of the most striking examples of Congress seeking to enforce the rule of law in recent years occurred when Congress investigated the murder of four Americans in Benghazi, Libya, on the night of September 11, 2012. The premeditated murders of the U.S. ambassador and three other American heroes were concealed by the Obama administration because the truth would have hurt President Obama's re-election efforts.

Just as the Magna Carta and the Glorious Revolution in 1688 guaranteed British monarchs would be held to the same laws as their subjects, the Constitution should have applied to President Obama—but, in practice, didn't.

Years after the attacks in Benghazi, the historical record is clear executive branch officials lied about the terrorist origin of the attacks, the failed U.S. military response, and the delayed law enforcement murder investigation. The motive to lie was also clear. The president's team wanted to conceal policy failures in Libya. Rather than acknowledge that American policy caused a leadership vacuum resulting in terrorist strongholds, the Obama foreign policy team placed Americans in grave danger while trying to create the appearance of peace in the region. When I joined Congress in 2015, the subsequent story I was privy to, while distressing, gave me hope the law applied to the "king" in America.

Clinton's False Narrative

Then Secretary of State Hillary Clinton was the chief proponent in the Obama Administration of the policy to take out Colonel Qhaddafi, the de facto leader of Libya, and topple his regime. Clinton viewed Libya as part of her own legacy, and her advisors frequently highlighted the overthrow of Qhaddafi in 2011, as one of her great successes as secretary of state.

But Clinton's self-promotion, and the success narrative she and her advisors built, fell apart a year later when our diplomatic mission in Benghazi came under attack and four Americans were brutally killed.

The terrorist attack began at 9:42 p.m., on September 11, 2012, and the threat continued for seven hours. The terrorists executed a plan, beginning at a U.S. State Department facility, and continued as they ambushed the Americans as they headed to an annex. The plan culminated with a deadly fire.

Immediately, President Obama, Secretary Clinton, and other senior officials were given detailed information about the attack, including the terrorists' weapons, the complexity of their attack, and the coordination of two attacks at separate locations. Clinton was armed with accurate and specific information about the attacks, yet rather than provide those details to the public, she created a false story, positing the attacks weren't the result of terrorism, but an organic burst of violence and protests in the Middle East instigated by an online video disparaging the prophet Muhammad.

In retrospect, we can see all too clearly Clinton's own statements—public and private—show how fluently she lied about the causes of the attack.

On the day of the attack, Clinton said the following in a public statement about the attack: "I condemn, in the strongest terms, the attack on our mission in Benghazi today…. Some have sought to justify this vicious behavior as a response to inflammatory material posted on the internet."[8]

It is clear that she knew then that this was not the case. That same night, in a call with the president of Libya, Clinton referred to the truth, about the role of a militant Islamic group, saying, "[O]ur diplomatic mission was attacked[.] …[T]here is a gun battle ongoing, which I understand Ansar as-Sharia [sic] is claiming responsibility for."[9] She did not mention an alternative scenario—be it a protest or a video—as the proverbial match that lit the fire in the region.

In an email to her daughter that same evening, Clinton was even more candid about the role of terrorism in the attacks, writing, "Two of our officers were killed in Benghazi, by an Al Queda-like [sic] group[.]"[10]

Again, no mention of a video.

The following day, September 12, in a public statement, Clinton was back to peddling the fabrication of the video prompting the violence, saying, "We are working to determine the precise motivations and methods of those who carried out this assault. Some have sought to justify this vicious behavior, along with the protest that took place at our Embassy in Cairo yesterday, as a response to inflammatory material posted on the internet."[11]

That same day, in a private statement, Clinton was more forthcoming with the Egyptian prime minister, saying, "We know that the attack in Libya had nothing to do with the film. It was a planned attack—not a protest…. Based on the information we saw today, we believe the group that claimed responsibility for this was affiliated with al Qaeda."

Such was the definitive and clear information from someone who was still lying to the American public.

The following day, Clinton again made a false public statement, this time in Morocco: "I also want to take a moment to address the video circulating on the internet that has led to these protests in a number of countries. To us, to me personally, this video is disgusting and reprehensible…. As long as there are those who are willing to shed blood and take innocent life in the name of God, the world will never know a true and lasting peace. It is especially wrong for violence to be directed against diplomatic missions."

The most despicable of Clinton's lies took place at the remains ceremonies for two of the Americans who died in the attack. According to the father of one of the victims, Tyrone Woods, as he recorded in his diary, "I gave Hillary a hug and shook her hand, and she said we are going to have the filmmaker arrested who was responsible for the death of my son." Even at the ceremony for a fallen American, Clinton chose to lie to the face of a grieving father.

The mother of Sean Smith, another American killed in the attack, recalled, "We were nose-to-nose at the coffin ceremony. [Hillary Clinton] told me it was the fault of the video. I said, 'Are you sure?' She says, 'Yes, that's what it was...it was the video.'"[12]

Conclusions from Congress

After extensive hearings and investigations, members of Congress were able to draw conclusions about the tragic events of September 2012. The U.S. military never reached Benghazi during the attacks, despite the prolonged period of the assault, because the Obama administration failed to send in troops or the weapons and armored vehicles necessary to protect the diplomatic mission.

The American people expect their government to take every step necessary to help those we put in harm's way. The U.S. military never did anything to rescue those attacked in Benghazi, leaving them to defend themselves against overwhelming forces. In contradiction to the Obama administration's assertions no one was able to land in Benghazi in time to help, the truth is the administration never even directed our military to save our own people in Benghazi.

What Difference Does It Make?

During a Senate hearing about the Benghazi attack, Hillary Clinton responded to a question from Senator Ron Johnson, with a revealing and flippant question of her own: "With all due respect, the fact is, we had four dead Americans. Was it because of a protest, or because of guys out for a walk one night who decide to kill some Americans? What difference, at this point, does it make?" She then went on to say, "It is our job to figure out what happened, and do everything we can to prevent it from ever happening again, Senator."[13]

Clinton was right about one thing, that it was the federal government's job to figure out what happened, in an effort to prevent something similar from ever happening again. She was wrong, however, that the underlying cause made no difference. She knew well the underlying *why* of the event mattered a great deal. It mattered to the American people. It mattered to the families who lost loved ones. And it certainly mattered for her career and legacy. She went to great lengths to fabricate a story about a video igniting violence, knowing it wasn't true, knowing it was terrorism, and then she repeated that story at every opportunity in an effort to conceal the truth, because she knew just how much of a difference it would make if the American public knew the full story.

In the absence of oversight and accountability from Congress, Clinton might have gotten away with it, perpetuating the lie that an internet video caused the attack. The secretary of state is, lest we forget, an unelected position. The founders anticipated this dilemma, handing Congress the authority to provide oversight and conduct investigations.

George Mason, one of our founders from Virginia, said at the Federal Convention, members of Congress "are not only Legislators, but they possess inquisitorial powers. They must meet frequently to inspect the Conduct of the public offices."[14] Clinton's shameful cover-up attempt in the wake of four Americans being murdered is exactly why our founders made sure to empower Congress with "inquisitorial" and investigative powers. The lessons of Clinton's betrayal of the public trust are laid bare: Undermining the rule of law undermines individual liberty. Our republican system requires individual liberty, which in turn, requires the rule of law. The founders' decision to make the legislative branch the preeminent branch of government was much more than an administrative style of organizing government powers; it was an absolute necessity to protect individual liberty.

CHAPTER 3

Checks and Balances

"Hence a double security arises to the rights of the people.
The different governments will control each other,
at the same time that each will be controlled by itself."[1]

—JAMES MADISON

The echo of gunfire crackled on the streets. Military and tribal militias clashed. Blood was spilled after an uprising led to a ruler's ouster following more than three decades in power. Hundreds of unarmed protesters were left for dead. Airstrikes left large swaths of the landscape in rubble in one of the poorest countries in the Arab world, a nation racked with unemployment and deadly political intrigue. One question persists: why was the United States involved in an intractable conflict on the other side of the globe?

A civil war in Yemen, at first glance, may not appear connected to the U.S. Constitution, but our military's involvement in that conflict is a good example of how our constitutional system of checks and balances should work.

Back in 2011, during the Arab Spring uprising—a series of antigovernment protests spreading across the Middle East—Yemen's authoritarian president was forced to step down and hand over power to his vice president Abdrabbuh Mansur Hadi, who assumed power in February of 2012. From day one, he struggled to control jihadist attacks. He was also unable to manage the separatist movement in the south of his country. Other problems plagued Yemen, including widespread corruption, which threatened every societal institution.

Throughout the uprisings, Iran has militarily supported the separatists. On the other side, the United States, United Kingdom, and France have aided Saudi Arabia in its effort to restore the Yemeni government next door. Military support from the United States has included aerial refueling, as well as military training designed to minimize civilian casualties, and intelligence sharing.

The United States has, by any definition, been engaged in the civil war in Yemen. There's no other way to put it. The problem is our involvement was never approved by Congress—and that is not the way it was supposed to be under our Constitution. Congress has never approved the use of our military for this war, despite the Constitution's clear requirement that the president must obtain approval from Congress before engaging in war.

By the time voters sent me to Congress in 2014, we as a nation were involved in the Yemeni conflict. I read the headlines, so I was not surprised. But I was offended by our involvement.

What it came down to, when I spoke to my congressional colleagues and others in the know, was this: Our country's involvement wasn't centered on an ostensible concern about terrorism. We were helping to fight a proxy war because Saudi Arabia was one of our key allies in the Middle East. What's more, the U.S. administration was keen on maintaining stability in the region, given our longstanding abiding need to minimize the impact of one of our sources of energy—oil.

The truth is, if it came to a congressional decision, after understanding the administration's position, I may have voted for intervention.

The problem is it never did.

On any given day, the United States is plunged in conflicts all over the world in varying degrees, and it's wrong for Americans to be engaged in so many clashes that don't belong to us.

I don't believe in isolationism. I do believe we ought to be careful about when we get involved. Every time Republicans want to spend a dollar on military, it seems liberals want to spend a dollar on social programs. And the end result is our bloated debt, which is plain bad fiscal policy.

Even more, it's a violation of our Constitution. The founders took a hard look at the world, and they sought to make sure we didn't overextend

ourselves, for Congress to check the executive branch from rushing head-long into conflict.

A subtle reminder hangs in oil on canvas in the rotunda of the U.S. Capitol: the Surrender of General Burgoyne. With the American flag fluttering prominently, the portrait depicts the British surrender at Saratoga, New York, a key inflection point in the American Revolution presaging French intervention on our side.

Having lived through this experience, and understanding the costs—both human and financial—of war, the founders carefully designed a system in which Congress would deliberate the necessity of military action before committing our Armed Forces.

War and Consent

In breaking from the British crown, our founders made the deliberate choice to put the decision to go to war in the hands of the legislative branch, rather than in the hands of the executive. The founders wanted to ensure the presidency would not morph into a power similar to that of the British king. Placing the war powers authority with Congress was one way of creating for the president of this new country a distinct role from the British monarch.

Our nation's founders understood that going to war is one of the most consequential decisions a nation ever makes. Because the legislative branch would be a more thoughtful and slow-moving body than the executive branch, where the president could act alone, the founders empowered the legislature with the authority to decide if and when to go war, as well as the oversight authority of other military actions.

Even Alexander Hamilton, who often argued in favor of a strong executive, advocated for a more limited role for the president to play in the arena of war. He preferred to give Congress the sole power to declare war. He wrote, in 1801: "The Congress shall have the power to declare war; the plain meaning of which is, that it is the peculiar and exclusive duty of Congress, when the nation is at peace, to change that state into a state of war...."[2]

Hamilton, after all, was all too aware of the cost of war, saying, "What are the chief sources of expense in every government? What has occasioned that enormous accumulation of debts with which several of the European nations are oppressed? The answer plainly is, wars and rebellions; the support of those institutions which are necessary to guard the body politic against these two most mortal diseases of society."[3]

But the "exclusive" duty of Congress Hamilton referenced to declare war has become blurred in recent decades, as presidents have taken that responsibility upon themselves.

As the father of a West Point graduate and a former Army officer who recently left the service, I have often thought about the genius of our founders' decision to give the war-making authority to the legislative branch, rather than to the president. Sometimes the slow-moving nature of Congress frustrates me, especially when there are problems with such commonsense solutions awaiting our action. Not the least of those is the dire consequences of not addressing our out-of-control national debt. However, I have come to appreciate in the instance of war, the founders not only anticipated the slowness of Congress, but they were counting on it. Congress owes it to every mother or father with a child in the Armed Forces to debate and carefully consider our military engagements. Our Constitution demands it, and our military deserves it.

War Powers Resolution

Over the past century, presidents have consistently taken it upon themselves to engage in war and trample on the Constitution's separation of powers. In the early 1970s, Congress took a step to check the president's power grab. Congress passed the War Powers Act, a congressional resolution to limit the president's ability to launch military actions abroad. The resolution, which passed Congress in 1973, was promptly vetoed by President Richard M. Nixon. Congress overrode his veto, and the resolution was enacted that November.

In a nutshell, the War Powers Act requires the president to notify Congress after deploying the Armed Forces, and limits how long military units can remain engaged in combat without congressional approval. The Vietnam War was the inspiration for this congressional initiative, as members of the House and Senate sought to avoid another lengthy military conflict.

When a bill is brought up under the War Powers Act, it is privileged business in the House and the Senate, which simply means it is guaranteed a vote on each chamber's floor, and the majority party is unable to block or stall a vote on it. At least, that is how the War Powers Act was intended to work.

Wolves and Political Games

In the fall of 2018, I sat in the Senate Radio Gallery, feeling perturbed as I participated in a press conference to announce an unusual bipartisan coalition I had helped build. On one side were liberals who opposed the war in Yemen on the grounds it was creating a humanitarian crisis, and they were generally opposed to U.S. military intervention. On the other side were me and my Republican colleagues who were concerned about enforcing the constitutional mandate requiring Congress, not the president, to engage in war.

Here was one of those rare opportunities when people from both sides of the aisle have different mindsets but a common goal: to require congressional control over war-making decisions.

At the press conference, I remember hearing nonsense from one particular liberal who intoned a concern the poor folks of Yemen would peer up into the sky and witness Saudi Arabian bombs identified with these letters: U.S.A. My first reaction was—and I was tempted to say it at the press conference—once the bombs exploded, the folks below wouldn't hold a grudge for too long. There are, let's not forget, times when valid reasons compel us to engage in war.

With this unlikely coalition, Congress faced the historic opportunity to use the War Powers Resolution to end the war in Yemen. The bipartisan coalition began working on an effort to direct President Trump to remove U.S. Armed Forces from the hostilities in Yemen. House Concurrent Resolution 138 was the bipartisan measure Congressman Ro Khanna, a Democrat from California, introduced to end U.S. involvement in the war in Yemen.

Because Congressman Khanna's Yemen bill was introduced under the War Powers Resolution, the bill was privileged and required a quick-turnaround vote. But it was only a matter of time before the leadership in the House devised a ploy to deprivilege the resolution—to kill it. When Congress reconvened after the 2018 election, after the Republicans lost the election but still held the majority until the new Congress was sworn into office that January, Republicans moved to derail the Yemen resolution.

Using the last few days of its majority power, the Republican leadership allowed the Rules Committee to maneuver to get rid of the Yemen War Powers. They quietly stuffed language blocking a floor vote, on whether to direct the president to end the Yemeni conflict, into an unrelated bill about, of all things, wolves. The Manage Our Wolves Act, a bill to remove the gray wolf from the endangered species list in the contiguous forty-eight states, had nothing to do with war powers or Yemen. But it was the bill Republican leaders chose to kill the War Powers Act vote on Yemen. And the House approved the wolf measure, blocking a vote on the Yemen resolution.

Republicans in House leadership may have thought they were simply using clever procedural machinations to avoid a difficult vote on an issue related to war, but in reality, they were doing something with serious constitutional consequences. By killing the Yemen resolution, the House leadership denied members the opportunity to vote on the floor of the House of Representatives, on whether or not the United States should be engaged in the Yemeni war.

By playing political games with a bill about wolves, the Republicans were able to skirt the important nature of the War Powers Resolution, and dodge their Constitutional responsibility to authorize and oversee war.

Not that I was ready to give up. Several months later, in June of 2019, I co-founded a new bipartisan War Powers Caucus, whose purpose is to reaffirm Congress's duty on matters of war and peace.

"We have allowed this power to atrophy, turning over decision-making to the executive," I announced. "I look forward to working with this group of lawmakers to reclaim our legislative authority over war-making activities, for the sake of our men and women in uniform."[4]

War and Peace in the Capitol

The political games surrounding the Wolves Act reminded me of Abraham Lincoln's reflections on why Congress must guard its war powers. Lincoln wrote on this topic in 1848, during his time in Congress, in the midst of America's War with Mexico.

"The provision of the Constitution giving the war-making powers to Congress, was dictated, as I understand it, by the following reasons: Kings had always been involving and impoverishing their people in wars, pretending generally, if not always, that the good of the people was the object. This, our [Constitutional] Convention understood to be the most oppressive of all kingly oppressions, and they resolved to so frame the Constitution that no one man should hold the power of bringing this oppression upon us."[5]

The concepts of war and peace aren't just memorialized in the wise words of Lincoln, but in concrete forms in the Capitol. In the niche to the right of the east entrance stands the marbled statue *War*, a male figure in ancient Roman toga and tunic, with one hand on the hilt of a sword, the other gripping the edge of his shield. *Peace*, cut in the figure of a female, stands in the niche to the left of the entrance. Bedecked in robe and sandals, she extends an olive branch to "War."

The statues are constant reminders to every member of Congress passing by that it is the legislature's role to allow the nation to engage in war. James Madison noted the highest wisdom of the Constitution could be seen in the clause giving the "question of war or peace to the legislature," rather than to the executive. As members of Congress were hiding behind

the wolves bill, War and Peace were standing in their places, ignored by today's politicians who have missed the wisdom of the Constitution's war powers clause.

Republicans are often guilty of giving into the executive branch's usurpation of our war-making powers. In July of 2019, I voted to approve legislation requiring the Trump administration to seek congressional authority before engaging in extended hostilities with Iran. In the moment, a Republican colleague sitting behind me leaned over my shoulder and asked why I was voting to embarrass President Trump. I wasn't. I was voting to abide by the Constitution, to require a House floor vote to authorize the use of military force.

We don't need another Wolves Act to scuttle our constitutional responsibility.

A Check on the Executive Branch

Our founders were prescient about what would happen if the executive branch expanded through increased war powers: more national debt, and less accountability to the legislative branch.

The Benghazi tragedy shows how right the founders were to fear an unaccountable executive branch. Congress, for decades, has turned a blind eye to the executive branch's use of the military. Hillary Clinton's brazen acts as secretary of state were the result of her hubris that Congress would have little oversight or heed in investigating the bloody Benghazi events.

Sometimes the clearest example for Americans to witness the system of checks and balances is in more run-of-the-mill events than war. The annual State of the Union Address, for one. That, of course, is when the president addresses Congress. These presidential speeches are televised, so every American can hear from the president about his policy accomplishments of the past year, as well as objectives for the coming year.

I have had the privilege of attending six State of the Union Addresses, delivered by President Obama and President Trump. It's impressive to experience the pomp and circumstance. But maybe not as much as you might think.

For one, some of my colleagues jostle for better positioning, placing a piece of paper in a seat closer to the center aisle to reserve a better spot to be seen on TV when the president marches down.

Actually, the TV cameras cause other problems. Heat, for one. With the bright lights aiding the cameras flooding the small space of the House floor, the temperature has a way of rising dramatically, causing a bout of congressional sweats among my colleagues.

This happens to be one of those rare occasions when members of Congress aren't in charge of our own chamber; we have to arrive early and can't leave until after the president's address.

This once caused quite a situation. In the lead-up to one State of the Union, I ventured out for some food and brought back some for a colleague who suffers from an allergy to grains. That means he can't eat flour. I brought a molten chocolate lava cake back for him, not realizing this could cause—how shall I say?—digestive issues. For about two and half hours, he squirmed in his seat, trying not to have an accident. I couldn't help ribbing him.

But on a more serious note, the State of the Union in recent decades has morphed into a spectacle, with the media trained on the president as a celebrity. What was he wearing? Did you notice his tan? What we get wrong in today's media mania culture, however, is the focus on the president, rather than the audience. The State of the Union address is supposed to be a reminder the president is constitutionally required to give an accounting to Congress. The Constitution says, in Article II, Section 3, the president "shall from time to time give to the Congress Information of the State of the Union, and recommend to their Consideration such measures as he shall judge necessary and expedient." Notice how the Constitution keeps the emphasis on Congress, the recipient of the information. Congress will then consider the actions to take, based on this report.

From 1790 to 1946, it was known simply as the "Annual Message." In 1942, it was informally called the "state of the union" address. But then in 1947, the message was officially given the name the "State of the Union Address."

It was President Woodrow Wilson who transformed the speech into what it is today. President Wilson was an advocate of a strong executive, and he made the address an in-person affair. For Wilson, the message to Congress provided a platform for him to present his agenda and rally Congress and the American people around his plans.

The result: the State of the Union today is largely unrecognizable from the way the founders envisioned it would act, as a check on the executive branch.

Washington's Example

In the rotunda of the Capitol hangs one of my favorite portraits, John Trumbull's "General George Washington Resigning His Commission." The grand oil painting catches your eye when you come across it. Washington stands under a halo of natural light. To his left sits an empty chair draped with ceremonial robes, representing one of American history's most important moments. That's when General George Washington resigned his commission as commander-in-chief of the Continental Army, on December 23, 1783, to the Congress of the Confederation, before becoming our nation's first president, in 1789.

Washington's resignation before Congress has had lasting significance in our nation. It was a surrender of power, which he was not under any compulsion to do. The portrait's artist, John Trumbull, wrote about the

moment in history, in his description for the art catalogue for Yale University, in 1835:

> *What a dazzling temptation was here to earthly ambition! Beloved by the military, venerated by the people, who was there to oppose the victorious chief, if he had chosen to retain that power, which he had so long held with universal approbation? The Caesars, the Cromwells, the Napoleons yielded to the charm of earthly ambition, and betrayed their country; but Washington aspired to loftier, imperishable glory, —to that glory which virtue alone can give, and which no power, no effort, no time, can ever take away or diminish.*[6]

It was a significant moment not only because of what he did, but also because of his audience. He resigned his commission to Congress, demonstrating the legislative body has oversight of the military. Washington's resignation also reinforced that we have a military with civilian leaders. The concept of civilian leadership has been one of the defining features of the American military system, and what distinguishes it from others, such as the British Royal Military. Civilian leadership of the military is another example of how our nation maintains the separation of powers in the war-making sphere.

CHAPTER 4

The Overreaching Executive

"The essence of Government is power; and power, lodged as it must
be in human hands, will ever be liable to abuse."[1]

—JAMES MADISON

As I step outside the House chamber on the second floor of the Capitol,
I guide my visitors halfway down the stairs outside, offering them a
sweeping view of the Supreme Court building and the Library of Congress.
That's when I call their attention to something else altogether—the crown-
ing achievement, literally, of the Capitol: the Statue of Freedom, perched
atop the dome, solitary, magisterial.

It is perhaps the most recognizable feature of the Capitol, an iconic
world image of liberty and government by the people. Peering into the
distance nearly three hundred feet above the East Front Plaza, the bronze
statue is of epic dimensions, soaring almost twenty feet high and weighing
about fifteen thousand pounds. Freedom is decked out in elaborate head-
dress topped by an eagle head and feathers. Her flowing dress is cinched
with a large broach emblazoned with two letters: U.S.

In her right hand, she clasps a sheathed sword, while the other clutches
a laurel wreath of victory and shield.

The Statue of Freedom perched atop the Capitol is something to behold
and serves as a symbol of my stewardship as a member of Congress, which
is why I selected that image of the Capitol dome to adorn my letterhead.

This is what I want my constituents to see, to be reminded of, when I write to them.

The Statue of Freedom also symbolizes the personal quest for freedom of one man, Philip Reid, born into slavery in Charleston, South Carolina, in 1820. In one of the great ironies of American history, Reid, as a slave, was assigned the complex project of creating and placing one of the world's most powerful symbols of freedom on the most visible building in our nation.

I'll admit, I didn't know the story of Reid until after I became a member of Congress and got the lowdown on the history of the Capitol from those in the know.

But once I heard about Reid's remarkable story, I delved deeper, reading more about it online. I mention all this about Reid during my tours, and though not one of my visitors has ever known the story beforehand, they are surely glad to hear it. Slavery is a terrible stain on our history, but my guests are palpably proud of how far America has come since then.

The statue was commissioned in 1855. Thomas Crawford, an American sculptor, created the plaster model of the statue in Rome, Italy. After his death in 1857, his widow shipped the statue in six crates, and the model was assembled and placed in what is now Statuary Hall. The following year, Clark Mills, a self-taught sculptor, was given the task of casting Freedom. Mills started his business in South Carolina, where he purchased Reid for $1,200. Reid dismantled the model in the Capitol, cast the individual sections, and finally assembled and mounted the bronze sections atop the dome.

On April 16, 1862, as Reid supervised the creation of the statute's massive bronze sections, Congress passed the District of Columbia Emancipation Act, freeing thousands of slaves living within the district. That included Reid.

As a free man, he kept working for Clark Mills.

At noon, on December 2, 1863, under Reid's supervision, the top section of the Statue of Freedom was raised and bolted on top of the Capitol dome.

Many of the experts with whom I have toured the Capitol offered various explanations for the direction the Statue of Freedom faces. Some say Freedom faces east because every morning she watches the sun rise on America with a new day of liberty for all. Others say she faces east because the primary entrance to the Capitol is on the east side, or because most residents of Washington, D.C. at the time lived on the east side. Yet others suggest she faces east because European settlers came from that direction. I have a different theory. I believe Freedom faces east because the executive branch officials, who worked to the west and were responsible for the construction of the Capitol, didn't want her to see their unconstitutional actions unfolding behind her. Perhaps they harbored guilty consciences, or maybe they merely possessed a wry sense of humor. Either way, our country's most famous symbol of freedom has her back turned to the White House and the executive branch.

Had she been facing the other way, Freedom might have shuddered while witnessing the manifold examples of executive overreach, including when Barack Obama boasted, as president, how all it took was a "pen and phone" for him to circumvent the legislature and do whatever he pleased.

Why the executive branch is so prone to overreach is complex, but there are two underlying reasons to explain it. The first is what our founding fathers said is an inescapable reality of human nature—people aspire to more power, and the president is no exception. The second reason has developed over time. Congress, unwilling to make hard decisions, has increasingly handed off its responsibilities to the executive branch and ignored many of the instances where the president has seized more power and authority, in violation of the Constitution.

My good friend, Senator Mike Lee of Utah, has explained the problem this way: "This is of our own making. Congress has recast itself as a back-seat driver in American politics."[2] Mike has often made this all too accurate point; I know because Mike and I spent a lot of time together. We lived in the same Washington, D.C. house, near the Capitol, during my first four years as a member of Congress. We also attended prayer dinners together every Tuesday night, and when I introduced Mike at events, I always liked to kid. "Mike and I live together," to which he would clarify to the audience we simply shared a house.

What doesn't bring a smile to my face is the sentiment, though. Mike is right; Congress could do a lot more to make sure we hold the executive branch in check. But unfortunately, Congress chooses not to do so.

While the founders sought to guard against executive overreach, they couldn't account for the pressure brought to bear not just by those who want to expand their domain, but who demand party allegiance even above our nation's interests. There were times I spoke out against voting along party lines when they were inconsistent with our role as legislators—and I was attacked for it. In one instance, the Republican leadership objected to my opposition to a procedural vote. The way I viewed my vote, it was an objection to the legislative branch taking a subservient role. The leadership viewed it a different way, and as punishment for not toeing the party line, they tried to remove me as president of the Republican freshman class.

The leadership promptly called a special meeting. But when it convened early one morning, they didn't have the votes to oust me.

To people outside the Beltway, such petty behavior might seem crazy. But the sad thing is, it's commonplace in the Capitol. Many of my colleagues believe their job is simply to support the president, as party loyalists, not as members of Congress granted its special role carved out by the Constitution.

As long as I am honored to serve the people—and even after—I will continue to speak out against executive overreach.

President Obama's Expansion of the Presidency

President Obama provided the starkest example of the type of executive expansion our founding fathers feared. Obama acted as if the Constitution and Congress were merely obstacles he could circumvent. Rather than viewing the checks and balances in our system of government as a protection guarding individual liberty, Obama took the view that the Constitution provides mere suggestions, not firm rules, for the separation of powers and limitations on the executive.

Throughout his presidency, Obama showed a willingness to overlook the Constitution and resort to lawlessness to implement his agenda.

Perhaps nowhere was his lawlessness more on display than in the area of Obamacare, his signature healthcare takeover law. In February 2013, the Labor Department announced it would delay for an entire year the part of the law limiting how much people have to spend on their own insurance. Obama, in this instance, was rewriting laws, ignoring the Constitution's requirement that a change to an existing law requires a piece of legislation, not a presidential order.

Later that year, the Obama administration announced over the July 4th holiday that it would delay the requirement that employers with at least fifty employees provide insurance complying with federal regulations, or otherwise pay a fine. Again, Obama felt empowered to act outside the law. When rallying for Americans' support of Obamacare in 2009 and 2010, Obama made the promise, "if you like your healthcare plan, you can keep it."[3] But in the early days, when Obamacare was being implemented, insurers began cancelling millions of insurance plans that were not in compliance with all of Obamacare's onerous regulations. Sidestepping Congress, Obama held a press conference to announce Americans would be allowed to continue purchasing insurance plans even if they didn't comply with Obamacare requirements.

Obama also used recess appointments to avoid Senate confirmations. In January of 2012, Obama appointed three people to the National Labor Relations Board, along with the head of the Consumer Financial Protection Bureau. The only problem with Obama's "recess" appointments was the Senate was not in recess. The Senate was holding pro forma sessions every three days, and clearly was not in recess. The Supreme Court, in 2014, ruled—unanimously, it is worth noting—Obama's "recess" appointments to the NLRB were illegal.

This occurred shortly before I joined Congress, but it was all the talk on the campaign trail.

This, I told citizens, showed why we needed to send some people to Washington, D.C., to stand up to lawlessness.

Obama was so brazen in his end-runs around Congress he often bragged about his lawless activities. Noted columnist David Harsanyi put it aptly when he said Obama "justified his executive overreach by openly contending he was working around the law-making branch of government because it refused to do what he desired."[4] Obama thus reinvented a new concept in Constitutional government—the justification of expanding the role of the president, because the president wasn't getting his way through legal and constitutional methods.

Obama's famous remark that he had a "pen and phone" and could thus take care of most of his legislative needs himself sounds a lot like the behavior of monarchs, who could write their own laws.

As one of 435 members of the House, there wasn't much I could do on my own to stop Obama's runaway train of constant overreach. But we tried, as a Republican-controlled House, to curb his acquisitiveness through actions on spending bills and other legal moves. Not that they stopped the Obama administration from flouting the law to implement his agenda, even if it meant he took extraordinary steps to silence opposition to his agenda.

The IRS as a Political Weapon

In May of 2013, in an extraordinary admission, the IRS acknowledged it targeted groups, especially conservatives, with "tea party" or "patriot" in their names. This admission of wrongdoing came after years when conservatives, me included, wondered why our applications for nonprofit organizations were held up without any formal IRS response. Let's not forget, I served in government for a long time before I became a member of Congress, so I was familiar with the hallmark of government—inefficiency. I figured the IRS's lack of action on certain nonprofit applications was just more of the same—federal inertia. Heck, as a prosecutor, I took on false charitable organizations; I worked with various IRS agents. It never occurred to me the IRS was acting in a discriminatory or partisan manner, even with an application of which I was a part; in 2011, I started a group advocating for a balanced budget, but our nonprofit application was never approved or denied. When I made the discovery, I was stunned. The IRS admitted during a press conference that those applications from conservatives were improperly delayed and unnecessarily scrutinized.

Under the IRS's nonprofit guidelines, organizations may apply for certain charitable or nonprofit classifications. For example, groups qualifying as 501(c)(3) charitable organizations count their donations as tax-deductible gifts, under the tax code. On the other hand, organizations engaging in limited political activity, such as 501(c)(4) entities, are not considered charitable organizations for purposes of the donor's taxes, but these organizations are exempt from paying taxes. Our political system is full of 501(c)(4) tax-exempt organizations engaging on many issues, from free speech to tax reform to protecting unborn life. These advocacy groups are a vibrant part of our election system.

Obama's administration, however, worried some of these nonprofit groups would undermine his agenda. Groups identifying as "tea party," or focused on health care freedom, for example, were viewed as a threat to the Obama administration. The scheme was put in place to halt those groups by delaying (sometimes for years) their applications for nonprofit status.

In 2013, once the scandal came to light, Congress began investigating the IRS's abuse of power. The House Ways and Means Committee and the House Oversight Committee each conducted investigations. By the time Congress began investigating, though, the real damage had been done. Organizations that would have existed and contributed to the political discourse in the 2012 election were sidelined.

In the fall of 2017, then-Attorney General Jeff Sessions announced the government's settlement with hundreds of groups the IRS had targeted. In a statement, Sessions said, "There is no excuse for this conduct. Hundreds of organizations were affected by these actions, and they deserve an apology from the IRS. We hope that today's settlement makes clear that this abuse of power will not be tolerated."

The Obama Administration was not the first group of progressives to use the IRS for political targeting. President Franklin Delano Roosevelt's abusive employment of the IRS to target his political enemies is well-documented, and may have served as the template for the Obama Administration. Even Roosevelt's own son, Elliott Roosevelt, reflected later: "My father may have been the originator of the concept of employing the IRS as a weapon of political retribution."[5]

The IRS, because of the nature of its taxing authority, is particularly subject to abusive and overreaching tactics by presidents, and even bureaucrats who work there. After all, the IRS is in the unique position of collecting and storing personal information about most American citizens.

President Roosevelt raised the top income tax rate in 1935, to an astonishing 79 percent. The top estate tax rate rose to 70 percent. President

Roosevelt's expansive government programs under the New Deal required massive funding, and Roosevelt hiked Americans' taxes to pay for his initiatives. At the same time, as the IRS was growing to handle its new taxing responsibilities, Roosevelt began using the IRS as a political weapon to target his enemies.

That included Louisiana Senator Huey Long. As the Democratic governor of Louisiana, Long built a corrupt political machine based on promises of free stuff to voters, with high state corporate taxes footing the bill for those favors. Long also had a bad habit of taking kickbacks from service providers in his state.

Long supported the president, but over time he became critical of the New Deal programs, arguing they were inadequate. Long became so effective in his criticisms, he soon made it difficult for Roosevelt to get his legislative agenda passed.

In response, Roosevelt began searching for ways to punish Long. The IRS was a natural choice for the overreaching executive. Roosevelt sent IRS agents to Louisiana to investigate. Long's practice of taking kickbacks and bribes provided the IRS with ample fodder to pursue him.

At the same time Roosevelt was beginning to realize the power of the IRS to terrorize his political opponents, another rival came into his line of sight. William Randolph Hearst, the newspaper tycoon who opposed Roosevelt's political programs, was soon placed under investigation. The IRS investigation failed to produce anything, because unlike Long, Hearst kept honest accounting books.

Father Charles Coughlin, a priest with a radio show in Detroit, was another critic of the New Deal. In response, the IRS sent reports on Coughlin's personal finances back to the president. Roosevelt, not content to just use the IRS in the investigation of Coughlin, also recruited James Farley, the postmaster general, to investigate Coughlin's mail. Roosevelt personally oversaw the investigation, hoping to find evidence through Coughlin's mail or financial reports, but there was insufficient evidence to launch a formal criminal investigation.

Another target of President Roosevelt was Congressman Hamilton Fish, a Republican who represented FDR's home district in New York. Fish was another staunch opponent of Roosevelt's extreme agenda. Unable to help defeat Congressman Fish in his election, Roosevelt revisited one of his favorite tactics, an IRS investigation. The IRS alleged Fish owed $5,000 in back taxes. Fish took the IRS to court, and the case extended for several years. In the end, the IRS was unable to prove its case against Fish, and he prevailed in court. The real loser was the taxpayer who footed the costly bill, as the IRS dragged out the matter to cause maximum pain to Fish.

Undeterred, President Roosevelt launched a second round of IRS abuse directed at Fish, this time in the form of a multi-year audit. Once again, the IRS was unable to find any errors in Fish's taxes. When the IRS was unable to pin anything on Fish, Roosevelt asked the FBI, then headed by J. Edgar Hoover, to investigate Fish for "subversive activities" during World War II.

In each instance, Roosevelt felt empowered to use the executive agencies to threaten and silence his political opponents. Without robust investigations from Congress, future presidents will feel emboldened to engage in abusive targeting, much like presidents Roosevelt and Obama did.

Such tactics cause me great concern, especially when I contemplate what we are forced by law to reveal about ourselves to the federal government—deeply personal information about medical matters, foreign bank accounts, charitable groups to which we've donated, and more.

Just take a look at your tax return. Look how much information is at the government's disposal.

As a former federal prosecutor, I understand this at a profound level, having taken people to trial for not filing tax returns or filing false tax returns. It's one thing if public information is brought to bear against us, as in the case of a bankruptcy, which is a public process. But imagine your personal information, the disclosure of which is compelled by law, is used against you for political gain. That's a line that should never be crossed, and the founders never intended for the government to be used for such nefarious ends. Even more, the founders didn't intend to have an income tax at all; it was created with the limited purpose to pay off the debts of World War I, before it morphed into the gargantuan entity it is today.

As memorialized in our Constitution, the founders clearly placed the "power of the purse" in the hands of the legislature. We are reminded of our central role if we would only take a close look at one of the best-known paintings hanging in the U.S. Capitol—Howard Chandler Christy's bold rendering of the *Signing of the Constitution*—for all to see, in the east grand stairway of the House wing.

The Limited Executive: Coolidge's Example

A more elusive figure in the Capitol is that of President Calvin Coolidge, aptly nicknamed "Silent Cal," whose presidency stands in stark contrast to the Obama and Roosevelt presidencies. Though my tour doesn't occasion an opportunity to ponder a Coolidge statue or plaque, his presence is felt; Coolidge, one of my favorite presidents, was a committed conservative who believed the federal government should play a limited role. Coolidge also happened to shepherd us through one of America's greatest periods of prosperity, in the 1920s.

Coolidge was elected to office after the first World War, when the federal debt grew to ten times what it was before the conflict. The economic picture was bleak. The top income tax rate stood at more than 70 percent, and wages were not keeping pace with families' expenses. The classic Democrat response was, just as it is today, for more government intervention and more government spending.

Coolidge campaigned on fiscal restraint and sensible budgeting. He perfected the art of saying no to special interest groups.

During the catastrophic Mississippi River flood in 1927, Coolidge was under pressure to offer federal aid. Rather than resort to federal funding to address the problem, he sent Commerce Secretary Herbert Hoover to coordinate the relief efforts. He surprised many across the country when his response was the same when his own home state of Vermont was hit with flooding. His consistency in spending—or not spending—reflected his firm belief that taxing individuals more than was necessary was a form of "legalized bribery," as he called it.[6] Throughout his presidency, he advocated for fewer regulations and less involvement from the federal government. He viewed an expansive regulatory regime as a threat to individual liberty.

Coolidge remarked that one of the most significant accomplishments of his presidency was "minding my own business."[7] Coolidge's decision to keep the federal government out of private citizens' business contrasted with FDR's decision to use federal agencies to meddle in the private affairs of everyday Americans.

Unlike Obama, who employed the "pen and phone" method of circumventing Congress and the law, President Coolidge stayed within the spirit of the Constitution, even when he disliked the Congressional agenda. Coolidge was fond of using the "pocket veto," a type of veto Congress cannot override. This type of veto becomes effective when the president refrains from signing a bill—waiting until Congress has adjourned, and then taking no action on the proposed legislation, letting it die by inaction. Article I, section 7 of the Constitution spells out the functionality of the veto: "the Congress by their adjournment prevent its return, in which case, it shall not be law."

Coolidge's presidency is an example of how limited government should work. The presidencies of Franklin Delano Roosevelt and Barack Obama remind us of why our founders feared a too-powerful executive, and why Congress must take its investigative authority seriously.

The solution to overreaching executives is to reactivate Congress as an investigative branch. The only way FDR and Obama were able to exceed their constitutional authority was because Congress failed to exercise sufficient oversight and rein in the president.

Philip Reid knew a thing or two about exercising sufficient oversight. As the foreman in the casting of the Statue of Freedom, Reid stepped in when an Italian sculptor hired to assemble the five sections refused unless granted a pay raise. It was Reid who figured out how the pieces were separated and put together. He was paid $1.25 a day, though his owner received those payments, except on Sundays, when it was his own. Mills, the man who bought Reid, described him as "short in stature, in good health, not prepossessing in appearance, but smart in mind." Reid was a freed man by the time the last piece of the Statue of Freedom was assembled in December 1863. He went on to become a respected businessman, identified in census records as a "plasterer."

While a plaque to Reid resides not at the Capitol, but where his remains lie at the National Harmony Memorial Park in Landover, Maryland, his place in history—and on my tour—remains resolute.

CHAPTER 5

The Supreme Court: The Branch "That's Next to Nothing"

"Of the three powers [...], the judiciary is next to nothing."[1]

—MONTESQUIEU

While walking through the Capitol, we make a stop on the tour that surprises many—the Old Supreme Court Chamber. The room, designed by Benjamin Henry Latrobe, features an eye-catching ceiling with nine lobed vaults held by stone ribs, supported by heavy brick piers. The marvel is the institution of the Supreme Court, which has taken on such epic proportions in our lives, began in a small and humble abode—on the lowly ground floor beneath the legislative body in the Capitol. If it weren't for a sign on the door indicating this is where the Supreme Court used to hold court, you might assume it was nothing more than a storage area, which it once was.

This chamber has experienced many incarnations over its lifetime. The Supreme Court first convened here in 1810, when John Marshall served as chief justice, and remained in this room until 1860. After that, the chamber was converted into the Law Library. In the mid-1930s, the Old Supreme Court Chamber's purpose changed again, when it was used by the Joint Committee on Atomic Energy. The room was abandoned in the 1960s, but restored for tourists to visit it in the 1970s.

Today, what we see are the mahogany desks the nine Supreme Court justices used. Seven of those desks are originals. The chairs are mismatched and each is unique, as the justices chose their own chairs.

As a former trial lawyer, I am struck by the intimacy of the space; I never argued a case standing so close to an appellate court, which in this case would have been no more than fifteen feet from the justices of the Supreme Court.

I wouldn't go so far as to call the confined room a cramped dungeon. But the word that comes to mind is *claustrophobic*.

When I bring guests in, they need to squeeze into the narrow space, single file, and it's impossible to spend much time to appreciate the modest dimensions of the room because visitors are usually clamoring to get in or out.

When we do begin talking about this remarkable chamber, I am often asked about one feature in particular—the clock hanging over the west fireplace. That clock was installed in 1837, at the request of Chief Justice Taney—a judge whose lasting legacy, as we will soon explore, forever tarnished the Supreme Court.

Above the clock is a plaster relief with the figure of Lady Justice. This portrayal of Justice is unique in that she wears no blindfold. Seated beside her is the winged figure of Fame, who holds up the U.S. Constitution under the beams of a sun on the rise. Maybe it's poetic justice that the clock is so closely tied to the man who placed it there—Justice Taney—because it's as if time stands still here, a ghostly reminder of the worst decision in Supreme Court history, which deprived blacks basic rights.

For most first-time Capitol tourists, the real surprise is the Supreme Court used to convene in, of all places, the basement of the legislative branch's home. "Why would the Supreme Court have been in the Capitol?" a tourist will ask. "Isn't the judiciary a co-equal branch of government?" another will posit. Here, again, we have the opportunity on the tour to examine the myth of "co-equal" branches of government. It's a natural opening for me to point out to my guests the founding fathers were sensitive to charges of elitism in government, given their odious experience across the pond, and they understood the Supreme Court was the least accountable branch of government; it was, after all, comprised of a group of jurists given a lifetime appointment.

It isn't only tourists who are under the impression the judiciary is a "co-equal" branch of government. A quick look at the Supreme Court's website reveals the institution's own misguided interpretation, and the

text on the page even uses the term "coequal branch" to question why the Supreme Court was ever housed inside the Capitol. "Yet surprisingly, despite its role as a coequal branch of government, the Supreme Court was not provided with a building of its own until 1935, the 146th year of its existence," declares the Supreme Court's site.[2] If words could be indignant, I get the feeling these might be.

The court became enamored with its own unconstitutional expanded role. It is precisely why the founding fathers were so concerned about the weakness of human nature, foreseeing how each branch of government would seek to expand its role and domain. The Supreme Court has done a good job of that.

A Fittingly Humble Location

It is distinctly possible to walk by the Old Supreme Court Chamber without realizing the significance of its location within the Capitol. I make a point of asking everyone on my tours if they have ever heard about the Supreme Court's start in the Capitol. Not once, in over a hundred tours, have I gotten the right answer. That's because the idea the Supreme Court started out in the Capitol defies the popular notion of an independent judiciary, and clashes with the images everyone sees on TV of the opulent building on the east side of the Capitol—a classic Roman temple, if I've ever seen one—where the Supreme Court resides now.

The Supreme Court is the only court specifically mentioned in the Constitution, and the Old Chamber, though a relic of the past, should remind us of the founders' intentions for the judiciary—and their vision for the role the court should play in the new republic. On the tours, I explain the history of the court's location to show not only the shift in physical space, but also the major shift in the public's view of the judiciary. In 1860, the court moved to a new location—but still remained in the Capitol—to the former Senate Chamber. The Supreme Court was housed in the Capitol until former President Taft, then serving as chief justice of the Supreme Court, convinced Congress the court deserved its own building.

It's too bad Congress didn't recall its history. Even Alexander Hamilton, a stout supporter of an expanded federal government, envisioned, in Federalist 78, the judicial branch of the new government would be the weakest of the three branches.[3] That characterization challenges our modern misconception of "co-equal branches." Along with being the weakest branch, the judiciary would be "the least dangerous," according to Hamilton.[4] The founders, ever mindful that a too-powerful government would pose dangers to individual liberty, sought creative ways to limit the powers of each branch of the government.

According to the Constitution, justices on the Supreme Court would enjoy tenure for life, and would be appointed, not elected. At first glance, those two aspects of the court—no elections and lifetime appointments— might seem to increase the likelihood the court would become the *most* dangerous branch. After all, didn't the founders go to great lengths to ensure two-year terms for members of the House, six-year terms for senators, and elections for the president every four years? As the founders noted, elections would create accountability to the people, and regular opportunities for voters to weigh in and voice their approval or disapproval.

The judiciary, on the other hand, would be outside the political process. Justices would not serve at the direction of the public, nor would they answer to Congress or be subject to political firings, as judges in England were at the time.

Hamilton here again provides insight into the founders' thoughts. The Supreme Court would be the weakest branch because it would possess "no influence over either the sword or the purse" and would have "neither force nor will, but merely judgment." In Federalist 78, Hamilton borrowed from Montesquieu, the famous Enlightenment philosopher, who said, "Of the three powers [...], the judiciary is next to nothing."[5] It was precisely this feature of the judiciary—its "nothingness" in the realm of political power that made this branch the least dangerous to individual liberty.

Inventing Judicial Review

Let's take a step back in history. *Marbury v. Madison*, as you may know, is the famous Supreme Court case establishing judicial review, the power of the court to invalidate laws in certain cases. In 1801, William Marbury and three others, whom outgoing President John Adams appointed to be justices of the peace, failed to receive their commissions the night before Thomas Jefferson's inauguration. The presidential election of 1800 pitted President Adams, a federalist seeking re-election, against Thomas Jefferson, a Democratic-Republican, a party he formed, which pushed against the federalists' policies of centralized power. Power in Congress also changed with this election, as the Democratic-Republicans achieved majorities in the House and Senate.

Adams knew exactly what the change in power meant for his party's future. In an attempt to shore up power for the federalists before he left office, Adams appointed his secretary of state, John Marshall, to be chief justice of the Supreme Court. Beyond that position, Adams worked with the outgoing federalists in Congress to create several new judicial offices, which he filled, of course, with federalists. In his final act, on March 1, 1801, Adams stayed up late that night to sign commissions for the new judges, which Secretary of State Marshall notarized.

In a humorous irony of political history, Marshall failed to deliver several of those signed commissions, including the one belonging to William Marbury who Adams named to be a justice of the peace for the District of Columbia. Marshall, it seemed, had a bit too much on his plate.

The Jefferson administration, not wanting the Adams' appointments to stand, refused to deliver those four commissions. Marbury and the three others sued for a "writ of mandamus," a fancy term for a judicial directive that a government official perform a particular duty required under the law.

Three of the plaintiffs attempted to get the Senate to compel Madison, President Jefferson's secretary of state, to provide a copy of their confirmations, in March 1801. That motion, however, failed in the Senate.

What happened next altered the course of the Supreme Court.

The four Adams appointees sued in the Supreme Court, hoping to get a ruling that would compel Madison to deliver the commissions. Chief Justice John Marshall's decision has shaped the Supreme Court—in ways Marshall could never have imagined.

In *Marbury*, the Marshall court determined that it could not take action to restore the commission because the underlying congressional act that expanded the court's jurisdiction was, itself, unconstitutional. The court acknowledged, however, that Marbury possessed a legal right to his commission violated by Madison's failure to perform a ministerial duty. This case drips with irony because the new chief justice failed to perform the ministerial duty of delivering the commission to Marbury, and then bestowed his new branch of government with vastly expanded powers.

The bottom line: Chief Justice Marshall argued a legislative act is void if the Supreme Court finds it to be in conflict with the Constitution. In the decision, Marshall wrote, "It is emphatically the province and duty of the Judicial Department to say what the law is,"[6] thus drastically departing from the founders' vision for the judiciary. President Jefferson immediately understood the implications of the Marshall court's judicial activism, and he wrote in a letter to one of his staunch allies: "The constitution is a mere thing of wax in the hands of the judiciary, which they may twist and shape into any form they please."[7]

While *Marbury* was the beginning of the court's enlargement of its power, it was by no means the end of this dangerous progression.

The Court Redefines Its Role

The court case that often, deservedly, gets labeled as the worst Supreme Court ruling is *Dred Scott v Sanford*, the second time the high court used the power of judicial review. In this 1857 case, the court found the U.S.

Constitution's provisions related to citizenship did not apply to black people, whether the person was a slave or not.

Dred Scott, an enslaved man who lived in slave-holding Missouri, was taken by his owners to a separate region called the Missouri Territory, which included parts of Minnesota, Iowa, and elsewhere—areas almost entirely "free" under the Missouri Compromise of 1820. Once he was taken back to slave-holding Missouri, Scott sued on the grounds he had been taken into "free" territory and was thus freed.

In the Supreme Court's 7-2 ruling, Chief Justice Roger Taney ruled that Scott, as a black man, lacked the requisite citizenship requirement to be able to sue in federal court. The ruling invalidated the entire Missouri Compromise.

President Abraham Lincoln, who took office in 1861, rejected the logic and implicit judicial supremacy of the *Dred Scott* case. In his first inaugural address, he proved how astute he was in his reading of the founders' writings, and challenged the *Dred Scott* ruling. Lincoln questioned, "...if the policy of the government, upon vital questions, affecting the whole people, is to be irrevocably fixed by decisions of the Supreme Court, the instant they are made, in ordinary litigation between parties, in personal actions, the people will have ceased to be their own rulers, having, to that extent, practically resigned their government, into the hands of that eminent tribunal."

Lincoln's administration continued to operate under the Missouri Compromise, largely ignoring *Dred Scott*. The Lincoln State Department issued passports to black Americans, effectively recognizing their citizenship, as only U.S. citizens were eligible to obtain passports.[8]

Lincoln predicted what we have now: a Supreme Court—that eminent tribunal, as he put it—ruling beyond what it should. Mind you, the legislative branch could get something wrong, but go back and fix it if need be. But when the high court creates an entirely new right, it also creates a slew of unintended consequences the other branches of government will have to fix. It can only answer the question in a case brought before it. Judicial review, expansive as the Marshall court ruled, opened Pandora's Box, undermining what the founders intended and what is best for our system of governance—a court with a limited role.

The Progressive Attack on the Supreme Court

Fifty years after the Dred Scott decision, progressives launched a systematic attack on the Supreme Court, further reinventing the court's authority.

The progressives in the early 20th Century were inspired by the worldwide socialist wins. The Bolsheviks seized power in Russia in 1917, and Germany and France were regressing toward socialism. The progressives' platform was based on Karl Marx's premise of "scientific socialism," a theory arguing the historical inevitability of the socialist agenda. Those wins around the world reinforced their faith in Marx's theory.

While enjoying the success of their global revolution, the socialists nevertheless found a surprising amount of resistance in America—from U.S. citizens, but especially from the Constitution. As it became increasingly clear to the progressives the Constitution was a thorn in their side, thwarting their efforts, they became bolder in expressing their opposition to it. The American progressives were willing to abandon the Constitution in the pursuit of big government and greater control over individuals' private spheres.

Whereas Madison and Jefferson believed a government of separated powers would simultaneously protect against a tyrannical executive and promote a just government, many politicians and academics during the progressive era rejected this idea and argued the opposite. The progressive thinkers argued a more consolidated government would produce efficiency and enable the president, acting on behalf of the country, to pursue an agenda of social and economic fairness.

To understand the progressive movement's significant and lasting impact on American politics, it is first necessary to understand the movement's political philosophy and view of history. Progressives were inspired by the Enlightenment's ideas of human progress, as well as Darwinian evolution, which the progressives adapted to the social and political sciences. The progressives believed it was the government's responsibility to accelerate and facilitate natural progress. Referencing Darwin's theories, the progressives argued the Constitution was an outdated document that failed to evolve with society, and it no longer reflected the needs of the people. President Wilson, in his book *Congressional Government: A Study in American Politics,* attacked the concept of separation of powers as an archaic and unjust mode of governance.[9]

The progressives' choices to advance their agenda through non-legislative routes should hardly surprise us. The legislative branch, by design, was the one most accountable and responsive to the will of the people. The progressives lacked the public buy-in, and rather than do the hard work of gathering public support for their agenda (or worse, perhaps fearing their agenda would face entrenched opposition from an American public unwilling to forfeit individual freedom), they looked to the other two branches of government to enact their agenda.

This fervor to use the courts to enact the progressives' agenda was on full display in Franklin Delano Roosevelt's administration.

Packing the Court

President Franklin Delano Roosevelt's presidency was predicated on bigger government. To accomplish that goal, his administration needed to control the individual and employ the courts to that end. The Great Depression and the second World War offered the excuse for him to expand the presidency and role of the federal government. In a misguided attempt to curtail the effects of the Great Depression, Roosevelt set to work on a series of programs he called the "New Deal," establishing new functions and departments for the government, and forever expanding the role of the federal government in our lives.

Several of his New Deal programs, most notably the National Recovery Administration and several parts of the Agricultural Adjustment Act, were struck down by the Supreme Court as unconstitutional. Increasingly frustrated by the court, Roosevelt began toying with the idea of expanding the court to add justices with a more favorable view of his plans.

On February 5, 1937, President Roosevelt announced a controversial plan to expand the number of Supreme Court justices to as many as fifteen, ostensibly to make it more efficient.[10] Even his insistence on government "efficiency" echoed the progressives' entire agenda for faster-moving government, irrespective of the Constitution.

Congress, the Supreme Court justices, and the American public were all united in their opposition to the court-packing scheme. Roosevelt never went forward with the plan because two of the justices switched to a more favorable position on the New Deal programs, thus eliminating the need for Roosevelt to take the brazen step of packing the court. The reversal of those justices' opinion became known as "the switch in time that saved nine," because it preserved the court's membership at nine justices. Remember this, though. We will return, in a later chapter, to court packing as a grab for power today.

Misguided Hysteria: The Politicization of the Confirmation Process

Until the last century, most nominees received only a voice vote, without a hearing. The first public hearings for a judicial nominee were held in 1916, for President Wilson's nominee to the Supreme Court, Louis Brandeis. After *Brown v. Board of Education*, which struck down school segregation, in 1954, the public became increasingly attuned to judicial nominees, and hearings became commonplace.

In 1982, President Ronald Reagan appointed Robert Bork to the D.C. Circuit Court of Appeals. Once Supreme Court Justice Lewis Powell announced his retirement five years later, Reagan nominated Bork to fill the upcoming vacancy on the high court. Progressives of the day strongly opposed Bork because of his conservative views, and they launched a campaign to assail his character and his judicial philosophy. In the end, his nomination was defeated in the Senate by a vote of 58 to 42. I'll never forget how that happened. I was a young Congressional staffer back then, working on the Iran-Contra affair, when I observed the televised hearings—a forerunner to today's reality TV—and the profoundly unfair way in which Bork was treated. His awkward professorial bearing and scraggly beard didn't help his cause on television. When his opponents couldn't find a fair way to attack him, they did the next best thing: A Democratic operative got ahold of Bork's Blockbuster movie rental account. To their dismay, he wasn't watching anything risqué. Rather, he was watching vanilla G-rated films.[11] He was assailed for being boring. It was one of the first times I realized Washington was playing by different rules, where mob-like character assassination was the order of the day. Bork's greatest offenses was he wanted us to respect the Constitution.

Or maybe the worst thing was, he was grilled by a gallery of U.S. senators of ignominious character: One was a former KKK member. Another was a confirmed plagiarizer. A third left behind a woman not his wife to drown in a car wreck.

But sometimes details get lost in the megaphone of politics. When President George H.W. Bush nominated Clarence Thomas to the Supreme Court, his confirmation hearings began in September of 1991—and another vicious attack was underway. The questions at the hearing largely focused on Thomas' views of *Roe v. Wade*, as well as his thoughts on private property. Then Senator Joe Biden even went so far in his questioning of Thomas as to ask him if he believed the Constitution grants individuals property rights. Holding up a book by legal scholar Richard Epstein, Biden inadvertently revealed his own progressive bias against private property as he railed against the institution of private ownership.

Failing to derail the nomination of Thomas through the hearings, the progressives found one of Thomas' former colleagues, Anita Hill, who proceeded to accuse Thomas of making sexual comments to her. Biden reopened the hearings, and the FBI investigated Hill's accusations, interviewing Thomas and Hill. President Bush maintained throughout the investigation he had complete confidence in Thomas.

If history has proven anything about the Bork and Thomas hearings, it's that they provided the far-left activists with a roadmap to discredit and even derail nominees they did not like, regardless the facts. They employed the same tactics when, in 2018, President Donald Trump announced his second nominee to the Supreme Court, Brett Kavanaugh. Progressive groups attempted to derail the confirmation process. Liberal groups engaged in a coordinated effort to discredit Kavanaugh, portraying him as a threat to women's rights and abortion. Progressives warned he would end contraception, overturn Obamacare, and according to Planned Parenthood's dark outlook, usher in an era with "fewer rights" for America's young women.

Far-left organizations, not content to let the confirmation hearings play out on the merits of Kavanaugh's career and jurisprudence, introduced a false narrative that Kavanaugh engaged in extreme sexual misconduct and participated in gang rape parties. Numerous women presented their stories to the Senate Judiciary Committee, each telling a tale more absurd than the previous. As the Republican investigators working for the committee scrutinized the mounting evidence, they began to see holes and contradictions within the stories. In the end, one accuser even admitted she fabricated her entire account of an alleged rape in the backseat of a car, as a "tactic" to kill Kavanaugh's chances of making it to the Supreme Court.[12]

Eventually, after dragging Kavanaugh's name through the mud, most of the accusers denied their wild claims, admitting they fabricated the stories wholesale.

The progressives' hysteria surrounding Kavanaugh reflected their own misguided view of the Supreme Court's role—the idea it's a place where justices are able to throw out the Constitution on a whim, and are free to pursue a certain agenda where the personal beliefs of justices matter more than their fidelity to the Constitution. The left's meltdown over Kavanaugh was a result of the progressives' decades-long manipulation of the court's role in government.

Look at the hysterical warnings about what they thought Kavanaugh would do: End women's rights. End contraception forever. The left resorts to hysteria in a reflection of their own inflated view of what the Supreme Court can and should do. It is little wonder, when you look at how many times the Supreme Court has reversed its own opinions, why the Supreme Court's role is legislating rather than interpreting law. For example, in *Brown v. Board of Education*, the Court reversed its ruling in *Plessey v. Ferguson*, in which it allowed "separate but equal" provisions of state law as applied to public accommodations which legalized "whites only" drinking fountains, hotels, and other restrictions on where blacks would be served. The Court also reversed itself in the 1941 case *United States v. Darby*, outlawing state child labor laws which they earlier permitted in *Hammer v. Dagenhart*.

As a member of Congress, I can say with confidence the toughest thing about being in the public eye is not running for office, but protecting your family. I go into the field of political battle, used to—and expecting—verbal punches. What I found heartbreaking about what Kavanaugh faced was how his family suffered with him. What's more, he is a deeply religious man. He served regularly in a soup kitchen long before he thought he might be a Supreme Court nominee. He coached his daughter's basketball team. He's a great American.

From Least Dangerous to Most Dangerous?

Over time, the Supreme Court has transitioned from the least to the most dangerous branch of government, as it has amassed new and unconstitutional powers, such as judicial review and the prerogative of judicial supremacy. Americans today are correctly on guard against Supreme Court nominees who do not align with their own views of the Constitution, because the court has evolved so far from its intended narrow scope.

If we need a reminder of what the founders intended, all we need to do is walk over to the Old Supreme Court Chamber to understand the judiciary was never envisioned to be a runaway branch of government, with unelected and unaccountable justices empowered to discard laws.

Proposals are in circulation as of this writing to protect against progressive attempts to pack the court. One such measure is a proposed constitutional amendment to establish the number of justices at nine. The great irony is, we wouldn't need to protect against court packing if the court's power had not been so greatly expanded.

CHAPTER 6

Centralizing Power at the Federal Level

> "Of all checks on democracy, federation has been the most efficacious and the most congenial…. The federal system limits and restrains the sovereign power by dividing it and by assigning to Government only certain defined rights. It is the only method of curbing not only the majority but the power of the whole people."[1]
>
> —LORD ACTON

When official business is being conducted, the floor of the House chamber is off limits to everyone except members of Congress and their staff. Observers are restricted to the upper gallery, or balcony. By tradition, children under the age of twelve are allowed as well; I suspect this is the case because kids are less likely to disrupt House deliberations than the occasional obstreperous adult. Once the House has adjourned, I invite guests to join me on the floor. I like to joke it is much easier to get guests in the Senate because they do a lot less work over there.

I show my guests where the president stands during the State of the Union Address. Many of the guests want to climb up the stairs to the Speaker's chair, but I tell them it's off limits. In my mind, there are certain areas that should remain inaccessible, and the Speaker's chair is one of those. There's no accounting for mischief from someone who might want to whack the gavel; besides, this is kind of a sacred place, where presidents have held sway, and there should be respect for the seat.

In January of 2015, in my first blush as a member of Congress, I had the honor to sit in the Speaker's chair for the first time; it was after the end of our legislative business, on an evening of my freshman year in the House, and I was serving as Speaker pro tempore, or in the temporary capacity as chair of the floor. This was the time of day when I'd recognize my colleagues if they wished to make remarks on the floor; some, as you might imagine, could go on quite the long blue streak.

Governor Mario Cuomo of New York had just passed away, and Nancy Pelosi, then House minority leader, wanted to give a floor speech expressing her appreciation for his life accomplishments. She approached the microphone, and with a quip, gave the standard request, "Mr. Speaker, may I address the floor for one minute?" The irony was not lost on me that the then former Speaker of the House, who was responsible for shepherding through this chamber the massive spending increase required of Obamacare and other onerous regulatory burdens, was addressing me as "Mr. Speaker." I thought for a moment about apologizing and pretending, in a moment of mischief, that I had not heard and asking her to repeat herself. Not knowing if anyone in Congress had a sense of humor, I passed on my prank.

My guests get a kick out of that. After explaining to them how the electronic voting system works in the House, I direct the guests to look toward the ceiling for an unexpected reinforcement of early federalism.

The upper wall is surrounded by the cameos of all the world's greatest figures in the making and transmitting of laws. Moses, of all the images, is the only one exhibiting a full-frontal face, the rest in profile. Moses's face occupies prime real estate on the wall, with his gaze fixed on the speaker's seat. James 4:12 reminds us, even though we often refer to the Ten Commandments as "the Law of Moses," (the Bible also uses that expression), it was God alone who gave the law. In much the same way our rights are God-given, so is the inspiration for the law.

I also like to talk about Moses in a different context, apart from his role in giving God's law to the Israelites. Exodus 18:13-26 provides an overview of an early example of federalism, which Moses helped organize. Moses grew increasingly exhausted from being the central figure to solve all problems the children of Israel brought forward. His father-in-law, seeing how untenable this situation was, suggested Moses delegate authority to sub-leaders, who would head up groups of thousands, hundreds, and tens. Moses's time would be reserved for only the cases rising to the level of needing his attention to handle. This new system could be said to be the first federalist administration of governing human affairs. This way of organizing leadership encouraged local problems to be

solved at the local level and closest to the people affected by the problem—a key feature of federalism. Of course, this analogy is imperfect, because in our system of federalism, many of the most complex issues should be left to the states, not kicked upstairs to the central government, because the local laboratories of democracy can innovate best to solve problems.

The Tenth Amendment to the Constitution draws on the lesson of Moses. "The powers not delegated to the United States by the Constitution, nor prohibited by it to the States, are reserved to the States respectively, or to the people." I like to make the connection for tourists that, even on the House floor, where national problems and federal solutions are addressed every day we are in session, Moses's face is a quiet reminder that federalism and local governance structures are the most effective way of tackling problems.

The Design of Federalism

The founders crafted a system of federalism, a governance structure designed to protect people from an invasive central government. James Madison, in Federalist 45, outlined how federalism would operate, writing, "The [federal] powers delegated by the proposed Constitution ...are few and defined. Those which are to remain in the state governments are numerous and indefinite. The Powers reserved to the several States will extend to all the objects which…concern the lives, liberties, and properties of the people…."[2]

In other words, in the founders' view of federalism, states would govern more directly in individuals' lives than would the federal government. Madison's words are instructive. The states' powers would govern matters concerning the "lives, liberties, and properties" of Americans. That is, states would have primary power in the areas of the utmost importance in individuals' lives.

A popular idea today, which progressives like to foist on us, is federalism is a structure by which states act as the administrative agents for the federal government, simply overseeing the federal government's programs and agenda. In truth, federalism, properly understood, is the system by which the national government and the state governments hold the power to check the other, without controlling one another. As Thomas Jefferson wrote, "When all government, domestic and foreign, in little as in great things, shall be drawn to Washington as the center of all power, it will render powerless the checks provided of one government on another, and will become as venal and oppressive as the government from which we separated."[3]

One of the more obvious displays of federalism in the Capitol building are the two statues each state chooses to add to the national collection. Throughout the Capitol, there are statues bearing the name of the donating state. The tradition dates back to 1864, and the original authorizing law stipulates each of the states is allowed to commission two statues "in marble or bronze…of deceased persons who have been citizens thereof." The bill called on the states to honor citizens "illustrious for their historic renown or for distinguished civic or military services such as each state may deem to be worthy of this national commemoration." The statues today can be seen in Statuary Hall and elsewhere throughout the Capitol: of Samuel Adams, Robert E. Lee, Helen Keller, Will Rogers, Henry Clay, Jefferson Davis, Thomas Edison, Barry Goldwater, Huey Pierce Long, Daniel Webster, Brigham Young, Sam Houston, Dwight D. Eisenhower, Andrew Jackson, and others.

The statues reflect the different characteristics of the states. Each has its own unique characteristics and history. America's strength lies in her diversity, and the statues reflect the different perspectives of states formed by influences of weather, topography, industrialization, agriculture, urbanization, and immigration. As our name indicates, we are the United *States* of America, not simply geographic divisions that answer to a powerful central government.

The states' ability to choose two statues is symbolic of the two senators each state sends to the Capitol. The Constitution called for states, not individual voters, to select their two senators and send them to the Capitol, in contrast to the direct election of House members.

As I often share on my tour, those statues from the states also serve as a testament to another pillar of our republic—the Electoral College. In the same way states determine which statues to send to Washington and the way the Constitution called for states to send senators to Washington, so, too, does the Electoral College rely on the states, rather than individual voters, to select the president of the United States.

The Constitution's design for the Electoral College and the mechanism for selecting senators through the states reinforce federalism and help give voice to large and small states alike. The founders' plan for federalism has been altered since the Constitution was ratified in several ways, but nothing changed the role of federalism as much as the Sixteenth and Seventeenth Amendments.

The Progressives Struggle with Federalism

The progressive era, from the 1890s to 1920, was marked by an immediate clash with the system of federalism. The same features of federalism that appealed to the founders frustrated the progressives. Federalism, by design, empowers states to hold the federal government in check. Federalism also creates an embedded system of competition among the states. States can compete for businesses and residents through their regulatory systems and their tax codes. It is, after all, no great surprise retirees often move from high-tax states to states such as Florida, where no state income tax exists.

Federalism, however, is inefficient, and the impatient progressives could not be bothered with the different state structures. The progressives wanted to implement a new regulatory structure encompassing labor laws and health codes. Federalism required the states to take the lead in these areas, but the progressives had no desire to work with each state legislature to get their legislative agenda passed. They also worried that even if they succeeded in getting a majority of the states on board with more inva-sive regulations, businesses and taxpayers would simply move to the states that had not adopted the progressives' agenda, thus creating incentives to abandon the new regulations. Far better, they thought, to bypass the state governments and go straight to the federal government.

The progressives identified with the rise of scientific management at the close of the 19th Century and turn of the 20th Century. The country was advancing economically, thanks to advancements in science and technol-ogy, as well as efficient management. A new field emerged of technocrats, often engineers or specialized business managers, who helped operation-alize efficient business practices on a scale never before seen in the world. The progressives took note and wondered why those same principles of scientific management could not be applied to the political realm.

Under the guise of providing more freedom, the progressives adopted an authoritarian outlook on what the federal government should be. Gone were the days of James Madison's vision of the federal government steering clear of matters related to life, liberty, and private property, allowing the states to govern in those areas. With the rise of the progressive movement, every part of the economy and individuals' private spheres are appropriate areas for the government to impose itself.

The federal government would have to expand, and the progres-sives promised it would be through scientific managers who were better equipped than average citizens to tackle the complicated problems. A *New Republic* editorial published on July 6, 1918, revealed the progressives' elitist attitude with one remark: "The business of politics has become too complex to be left to the pretentious misunderstandings of the benevolent amateur."[4] The benevolent amateur here can be understood as the everyday American citizen, who, no matter how good his intentions, is ill-equipped to tackle problems with the expertise of the dedicated managers, according to the progressives' thinking.

Federalism was one of the biggest hurdles for the progressives in their attempt to create a nation managed by scientific experts. The founders chose the system of federalism because the structure would act as a brake on the federal government's ambitions to control more areas of individu-als' lives. The progressives inverted that reasoning, and wanting the federal government to take on a more active role in managing the private sector and solving problems, they jettisoned federalism.

Beginning in the late 1800s, progressives built the case for the government to assume new functions, even assuming the role of providing for individuals' economic security. The progressives dismissed the notion that human nature was fixed—a foundational aspect of the founders' thinking. Instead, they preferred the view that human nature was evolving along with history, and with it, government's purpose should change. If the new country, in the late 18th Century, needed a government with a limited scope and slow-moving checks on power, the economic realities in the 19th and 20th Century, the progressives argued, necessitated a robust, streamlined, and more efficient government.

Since the Civil War's end, the country had witnessed a slow increase in the federal government's regulatory reach in matters related to individuals' economic welfare. The Interstate Commerce Commission was created in 1887, with the passage of the Sherman Antitrust Act only three years later. The Food and Drug Administration came into existence in 1906, the Federal Reserve in 1913, and the Federal Trade Commission in 1914.

The unvarnished truth is, there is so much the federal government has grabbed control of that should be handled by the states. When the federal government asserted its influence in the wake of the Civil War, the bureaucrats just kept marching ahead, taking over less and less morally justified areas, beyond slavery, until we find ourselves with a centralized government ballooned out of control.

Paying for a Strong Central Government: The 16th Amendment

Two progressive goals intersected with one another and led to the federal income tax. The first goal was a pragmatic one—to find new revenue to pay for the expanded work of the federal government initially, or as a pretext to cover the cost of World War I. The second goal, however, stemmed from the social agenda of fairness—to redistribute wealth and compel the "robber barons,"[5] as the liberals of the day called the wealthy, to pay for their shiny new programs.

The progressive era emerged in response not only to the rapid industrialization in the United States, but to the overlapping creation of enormous wealth. John D. Rockefeller and others amassed huge fortunes, and progressives grew increasingly agitated about the wealth disparities in the country.

Teddy Roosevelt was fond of railing against the successful businessmen, and he felt that an income tax was the correct mechanism to go after some of their profits. The Constitution, however, stood in his way. The founders had already conceived of the dangers that would arise if the federal government had the ability to levy a personal income tax. Roosevelt and other progressives thus set their eyes on changing the Constitution to allow for such a tax.

The Sixteenth Amendment to the Constitution, which allowed for direct taxation on individuals' income, was ratified in 1913. Within just five years of the federal income tax's existence, the tax rate ballooned to 73 percent from 6 percent for top earners when the Sixteenth Amendment was passed.

With all this new money flowing to Washington, the government had little incentive to keep federal spending down. It is clear that constitutional amendments must have substantial public support to pass both houses of Congress with a two-thirds majority and three-quarters of the state legislatures. It is also clear Americans wanted an income tax and less federalism because they believed it would enhance their economic well-being without limiting their individual rights. Americans soon learned trading freedom for economic security results in neither liberty nor prosperity.

The national debt grew as a consequence of the expanded mission of the federal government, and because of the government's now-easy access to Americans' paychecks. As the federal government began to play an increasingly larger role in the private sphere, it should not surprise us the debt accelerated. In 1913, federal spending was 2.5 percent of gross national product, and our national debt was $2.9 billion.[6] Now we have a staggering $22 trillion-plus of national debt. What began as a supposed undergirding of American prosperity and equality may well prove to be its demise. Ask yourself what happens when a debt cannot be repaid.

The gross expansion of the federal government is immoral. There's no other way to put it. How can anyone take their role as an American in a republic seriously if our leaders act so unconscionably with the debt? While we enjoy a high standard of living today, we are saddling our children and grandchildren with the cost of our excesses. It is, as others have remarked, nothing short of generational theft and a denial of opportunity for future generations.

Stamping out the States' Voices: The Seventeenth Amendment

Just as the Sixteenth Amendment's introduction of a federal income tax accelerated the growth of federal spending and the federal government's reach, so, too, did the Seventeenth Amendment, which was ratified the same year. The Seventeenth Amendment introduced a new feature of democracy—the direct election of U.S. senators, which undermined a key aspect of federalism, as the founders contemplated, and altered the balance of power between the federal and state governments.

Prior to the Seventeenth Amendment, senators were chosen in accordance with Article I, Section 3 of the Constitution, which called for state legislatures to choose their U.S. senators. By eliminating states' voices in the selection of senators, the progressives were able to achieve two of their goals. First, they established a clearer connection between Washington and the individuals, bypassing the state governments and undermining federalism. Second, they were able to make the federal government move more quickly, without the need for states to give their consent.

Federal legislation must be approved by both the House and the Senate, another safeguard on liberty our founders devised. Prior to the Seventeenth Amendment, this arrangement meant legislation had to pass with the support of the people's representatives, in the House of Representatives, and with the support of the states' representatives in the Senate. The founders correctly saw how the states could act as an effective barrier to the federal government's plans, especially when those plans would inhibit individual liberty. The progressives, however, were convinced states were holding back the power of the federal government to be the driver of "positive" social change.

The Risk of Trading Liberty for Economic Security

Fundamentally altering the relationship between the individual and the federal government, the Sixteenth Amendment created a new taxing relationship between the federal government and the individual, and the Seventeenth Amendment eliminated the protections of the states' voices in lawmaking. The result of both has been unprecedented levels of spending and an increasingly invasive federal government, empowered to encroach on private property rights and intervene in private economic arrangements.

The progressives promised their agenda would usher in an era of greater economic security for individuals, but it has not worked out that way. States are now the recipients of vast sums of federal funds, and their role has been transformed into subservient administrative agents for the federal government, rather than as a protector of individual rights. States no longer serve as a barrier between the federal government and individuals; instead, they often work in partnership with the federal government.

In the name of increasing economic security, the progressives succeeded in increasing the federal government's reach into individuals' spheres.

The national debt, growing every day, is a stark example of the progressives' damaging impact. As of this writing, each U.S. citizen owes an overwhelming $80,000, and even worse, each documented U.S. taxpayer's share is close to $250,000. The debt continues to grow.

The people the progressives promised to assist with their new vision for government are those most at risk today. More than a century after the progressives reimagined government as the primary vehicle to bring security to every American, we see even more individuals left to fend for themselves. Look at what this movement has wrought: Vast numbers of people have become economically dependent on the government, in what can only be described as a breakdown of the family. The result of these damaging tax and welfare policies is the rise of societal ills with which we are all too familiar today: violent crime, property crime, illicit drug use, school shootings, homelessness, childhood neglect, single-parent families, fathers abandoning their filial obligations, you name it. There is something palpably wrong when the unintended consequence of the growth of government is, for instance, sending this message to a single mother—every time she gives birth, she will receive more government funds, as long as she doesn't have a man in the house.

The cycle of poverty was never more pronounced than in the sad tale of Tom Fletcher.

On April 24, 1964, President Lyndon B. Johnson visited the modest porch of a man who was to become the face of Johnson's War on Poverty. Fletcher was a thirty-eight-year-old elementary school dropout who subsisted with his wife and eight kids in Kentucky's coal country. Johnson and his entourage made a big deal before the assembled press about how, on that afternoon, he was declaring "a national war on poverty. Our objective: total victory."

Victory never arrived, not even partially. Fletcher was the beneficiary of various social welfare programs under Johnson's new initiative, working for federal government road crews, picking up trash. Ultimately, though, Fletcher ended up squatting on his porch, living off $282 in disability payments. He remarried to a woman who was convicted of murdering their three-year-old daughter and attempting to kill their four-year-old son to collect on burial insurance policies. It got to the point where Fletcher was tired of the periodic pilgrimages of the press to his home to find out whether the War on Poverty had ever lifted him out of poverty. "After all this time," he groused, "I'd think they would be letting it go."[7]

At the age of seventy-eight, he died in 2004. Since then, we have more poverty—and debt—than ever before. That's how effective big government programs are.

The Electoral College: The Last Vestige of Federalism

As we've seen, the founders crafted our system of government to include competition between the different levels of government. States would perform the role of holding the federal government accountable in areas of spending, regulations, and individual liberty. The Seventeenth Amendment began the process of undoing that accountability system. Modern-day progressives' plan to eliminate the Electoral College would pick up where the original progressives left off in their attempts to marginalize states' voices.

Article II, Section 1 of the Constitution spells out how the Electoral College is to function. States can select electors in any manner they choose, and in a number equal to their total congressional representation; that is, senators plus representatives. The electors would then meet and vote for two people to run the country, at least one of whom could not be an inhabitant of their state. Under the original design in the Constitution, the person receiving the largest number of votes, provided it was a majority of the number of electors, would be elected president, and the person with the second largest number of votes would become vice president.

The method for choosing the vice president changed with the passage of the Twelfth Amendment, in 1804. Support for the amendment arose after the 1796 election resulted in opposing parties winning, President John Adams, the Federalist, and the vice president Thomas Jefferson, the Democratic-Republican. The system again produced a less-than-desirable outcome in the 1800 election, with a tie between Jefferson and Aaron Burr.

Today, of course, vice presidential candidates are chosen by the presidential candidate, and the two campaign together as a package deal on the ballot.

As for choosing their electors, most states adopted a general system in which slates of electors are selected through a statewide vote. The winner of a state's popular vote also wins the state's entire pool of electoral votes. Only two states, Maine and Nebraska, have chosen to deviate from this method, instead allocating electoral votes to the victor in each House district, and then providing a two-electoral-vote bonus to the statewide winner.

Lately, some presidential electors have taken matters into their own hands. In 2016, three electors in Washington State voted for Colin Powell instead of Hillary Clinton, the presumptive Democratic nominee. Now I could, of course, understand their misgivings about Clinton, given what we've enumerated in previous chapters about her unsavory tactics as secretary of state. In this case, the state law required the electors to cast their vote for the party nominee, or face a civil penalty of up to $1,000. The three electors failed to vote for the nominee, and they were fined. Since then, they've appealed their case to the Washington State Supreme Court, which ruled against them, saying they were pledged to "act by authority of the state."[8] But the three electors are now asking the U.S. Supreme Court to address their claims, which they argue are backed by the Constitution.

"The original text of the Constitution secures to electors the freedom to vote as they choose," their lawyers argued in court filings.[9]

Progressives often charge that the Electoral College frequently allows candidates to win the White House with fewer popular votes than their opponent. Yet this scenario has only occurred four times—with Rutherford

B. Hayes in 1876, Benjamin Harrison in 1888, George W. Bush in 2000, and Donald Trump in 2016. In response, progressives argue the only remedy is to abolish the Electoral College and establish a direct popular vote.

The National Popular Vote initiative is the progressives' preferred way of dealing with the Electoral College. This proposal encourages state legislatures to pass legislation requiring their electors to cast their vote for the candidate who has won the national popular vote, irrespective of how the candidate fared in their own state. The language of the bill stipulates this new system for casting a vote for the national popular winner will not go into effect until the legislation is passed by enough states to change the outcome of the election. In other words, until the agreeing states have enough electoral votes to determine the election, this remains a reform-in-the-works.

Even presidential candidates are getting in on the action and attempting to do away with the Electoral College. Senator Elizabeth Warren, who was running for president in 2020, has been an outspoken advocate for abolishing the Electoral College. Other 2020 candidates who sought the Democratic nomination for president have followed suit and are advocating the same.

The Electoral College showcases the founders' genius. They correctly identified our nation's regional diversity as a strength and challenge. That challenge has only grown over time, as our country's borders have expanded far beyond the original perimeter of the new nation. The Electoral College helps ensure a farmer in a rural state can have a voice in the presidential election. Direct elections of the president, which progressives constantly tell us would ensure every vote counts, would in fact, have the opposite effect. Entire regions would lose their voice, and their vote and the president would be chosen by people living in only a handful of ultra-liberal cities. Candidates would bypass so-called flyover states in the heart of the country, in favor of currying a treasure trove of votes in liberal strongholds like Los Angeles and Boston.

As with most things the progressives attempt to push on us, abolishing the Electoral College sounds like it would strengthen our republic. Progressives disguise their real intentions with language of fairness and equality. Direct elections of the president, despite how progressives frame the issue, would wipe out the need for presidential candidates to visit or campaign in most states. Why bother? A trip to New York City or San Francisco is a better use of time for a presidential candidate in the absence of the Electoral College. As empirical history proves, voters in high-density population areas tend to be more dependent on government largess, and therefore vote to keep the government expanding. Democrats farm these areas to maintain and grow their power and control.

This hits close to home for me as a member of Congress representing a rural district, where citizens tend to be self-sufficient, are individual-liberty minded, and eschew government intervention.

If we do away with the Electoral College, the only folks in my state who would get a whiff of presidential candidates would be in, maybe, Denver, while many others would be ignored in the Rocky Mountain west, a region of the country that produces much of America's energy and yields a lot of food for our nation.

People in my district have already seen what happens when the one liberal bastion wields undue influence on the rest. Denver, given its vast population, imposes its liberal policies on other parts of the state, calling for restrictions on our Second Amendment right to keep and bear arms.

It's also Denver and its big city liberal energy policies that have driven up the price of electrical consumption in rural parts of the state.

The American republic has endured for more than two and a half centuries *because of* the institutions our founders put in place—not in spite of those institutions, as progressives would have us believe. Our founders chose a republic, not a democracy for the nation, because they knew it was the system with the greatest chance of ensuring freedom and prosperity. Republics encourage individual action, while democracies devolve into mob or collectivist rule.

What it comes down to is this: the more the federal government grows, the more our liberties shrink.

The more the central government covets power, the more it diminishes what the founding fathers intended for our local leaders, who knew what was happening on the ground, who knew how to solve local problems with local solutions.

When, for instance, the federal government took control of education policy in the United States, the local school board became obsolete. And while the national government was dictating what a kid in Brooklyn should learn, it overlooked the notion that a kid in rural Colorado maybe needed to learn something else—about Colorado history, about the accomplishments of the Native Americans on the plains, about religious persecution of Mormons as they traveled west.

When we remove local control, we lose something else; we lose people's connection to our nation. They become less patriotic. They become less willing to fight our wars. They become less willing to sacrifice in the shadow of recession because they don't feel included.

A relative once told me that Greeley, Colorado, some fifty years ago, was the kind of place where well-respected citizens took it upon themselves to run the town. That included the bank president, the guy who owned the feed lot, and others who cared about their roots. Their concern was based on a biblical understanding that when much is given, much is expected. It was a calling to shepherd their town to prosperity. Now with the steady incursions of progressives and their bloated government programs, we are left with towns bereft of local leaders, places that have a heck of a time finding someone to run for the school board, for the city council. Sometimes the situation is so bad a candidate won't have to run because there is no opponent. This is not what our founders envisioned in erecting our republic.

CHAPTER 7

Two Rights Essential to Republican Government

"Liberty is meaningless where the right to utter one's thoughts
and opinions has ceased to exist."[1]

—FREDERICK DOUGLASS

One of my favorite quotes, inscribed on the wall of the Cox Corridors in the Capitol, was also one of Benjamin Franklin's favorite quotes. He borrowed it from *The London Journal* and reprinted it in his *New England Courant*: "Without Freedom of Thought, there can be no such Thing as Wisdom; and no such Thing as publick Liberty, without Freedom of Speech."[2] For Franklin and the other founding fathers, there was a vital and inseparable link between liberty and freedom of speech.

The Revolutionary War was the result of revolutionary ideas, and the founders knew freedom of speech and freedom of press would be essential for buttressing those ideas for future generations. It is no coincidence our founders took part in various aspects of educating the public, from writing the documents explaining the American experiment in self-government to establishing institutions to guarantee the exchange of those ideas.

Thomas Jefferson founded a university, the University of Virginia. Thomas Paine turned the political pamphlet *Common Sense* into a near art form. Franklin, meanwhile, was occupied with two forms of idea

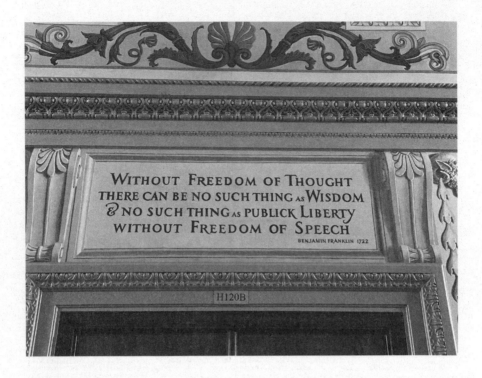

WITHOUT FREEDOM OF THOUGHT
THERE CAN BE NO SUCH THING AS WISDOM
& NO SUCH THING AS PUBLICK LIBERTY
WITHOUT FREEDOM OF SPEECH

BENJAMIN FRANKLIN 1722

H120B

circulation—the creation of the lending library and the newspaper he founded, *The Pennsylvania Gazette.* Furthermore, the founders, having written the Constitution, arguably the most important political document in human history, didn't leave it at that. They turned their attention next to writing eighty-five essays to explain the rationale for each feature of our republican form of government.

Our founders went to great lengths to put ideas into public circulation because they knew a republic *of* the people and *for* the people would require accountability *to* the people, as well as ongoing input from the people. Freedom of speech and freedom of the press, enshrined in the First Amendment to the Constitution, are the best ways to guarantee accountability and input.

I understand this at a deep level as a public figure who is also a public speaker involved in the marketplace of ideas; this is what I've chosen to do for a living, and I appreciate what the founders imparted; that you can't have freedom without free speech—all kinds of speech. I'm reminded of a recent meeting, a private business gathering. I was talking with some attendees about China, and someone opined that China is an economic force; how it's investing in Africa, how it's making smart moves.

And yet I knew there was little to worry about. China could not achieve its full potential without giving its people more freedom. Because a country can't thrive unless there is protection for people's freedoms, unless people can speak out, and in China such freedom is a threat to the government. We create because we have the freedom of speech, which leads to the freedom of ideas, which leads to the freedom of innovation.

The only thing that can hold us back from freedom is when the thuggery of the today's progressives seeks to clamp down on free speech. Speech they dislike is labeled hate speech, racist, or some other pernicious -*ist*. In their corrupted world, no room resides for a difference of opinion.

Republican Necessities

Freedom of the press and freedom of speech are much more than liberties for individuals to enjoy. These two related freedoms are necessary for a republican form of government to survive, and the beneficiaries of these freedoms include the public, not simply those exercising their rights. The hallmark feature of a republican government is public influence over implemented laws. This type of government must encompass the will of the people and take into consideration the people's concerns about proposed legislation. It is fascinating for us to consider how the founders envisioned the role between the individual and the collective. The founders saw that rights, including fundamental rights, such as the right to free speech and freedom of the press, first benefit the individual, but then the benefit is felt far and wide within the whole of society. Progressives like to invert that relationship and assure us individual rights will flow from their practice of first looking to the collective. But that is never how it pans out in practice.

The Bill of Rights was a product of the republican style of input our founders anticipated. At first, Madison opposed the inclusion of a Bill of Rights in the Constitution, not because he disagreed with the rights, but because he thought it was unnecessary to spell them out in the Constitution. He was tasked with editing the Bill of Rights, with feedback from the ratifying conventions. The Bill of Rights was not a decree handed down to the people; it was a product of the public will and the people's input.

Freedom of Speech: "The Real Sovereign"

Let's return to the statue of Ronald Reagan, which serves as a good reminder of the importance of free speech. Reagan's sense of humor helped define some of the weightiest matters of the day. Reagan often shared versions of this joke: An American is speaking with a Soviet citizen and says, "In America, we have freedom of speech. I can stand outside the White House and yell, 'Down with Reagan!' without being punished." The Soviet citizen is unimpressed. "So? We have freedom of speech in the Soviet Union as well. I can stand outside the Kremlin and yell, 'Down with Reagan!' without any concern of being punished."

The joke illustrates a key feature of the vast reach of our freedom of speech in America—we have a right to say what we want, even when our ideas clash with the government's position or the president's views.

Reagan was a fierce proponent of free speech, especially political free speech, because he understood the power of words to hold government in check and safeguard liberty—and even bring down totalitarian regimes. He also saw the interconnectedness of all freedoms. Freedom of religion doesn't matter without the freedom to live out one's faith in daily life. Freedom of the press is similarly hollow without the corresponding freedoms to criticize the government without fear of retribution. Similarly, the right to private property is meaningless without the right to defend that property, even from an encroaching government.

In dealing with the Soviet Union, Reagan resembled an earlier president—Madison. Writing anonymously in the *National Gazette,* in 1791, Madison offered this wisdom: "Public opinion sets bounds to every government and is the real sovereign in every free one."[3] The Soviet government brutally restricted speech because speech has the power to shape public opinion, which in turn, sets limitations on the government.

As Frederick Douglass noted, "Liberty is meaningless where the right to utter one's thoughts and opinions has ceased to exist. That, of all rights, is the dread of tyrants. It is the right which they first of all strike down."[4] It is no coincidence totalitarian regimes move swiftly to rein in free speech.

As a member of the House Foreign Affairs Committee, I am all too familiar with the heavy hand of totalitarianism in other parts of the globe. Closest to our shores is Cuba, where people are punished for speaking out, beaten by authorities. Venezuela's collapse has been marked by political corruption, unemployment, and violence in the streets, leaving dead bodies, courtesy of leftist paramilitary goons who terrorize the countryside with extortion, kidnapping, and murder. Further afield, Russia's autocratic president, Vladimir Putin, has allegedly ordered the assassination of political opponents.

It was Reagan who hoped for a different future for the former Soviet Union, saying, "Your new leaders appear to grasp the connection between certain freedoms and economic growth."[5]

Harkening to our freedom, the president added, "We hope that one freedom will lead to another, that the Soviet government will understand that it is the individual who is always the source of economic creativity."[6]

Evidently, some of our own politicians have failed to heed Reagan's inspiration about the product of freedom.

Not long ago, in the fall of 2019, Gov. Jared Polis of Colorado was accused of having his staffers request unflattering stories about him be removed from at least three Colorado newspapers.[7]

The newspapers refused, with one editor remarking, "Very surprised you would make such a request."[8]

I have to admit, I was amazed myself. I've called newspapers to seek a correction when I was misquoted, or if there was an inaccuracy in an article. But I'd never dare to order a story be removed.

It's not how we do things in America.

Obama's Attempt to Silence Free Speech

President Obama, by contrast, did not share Reagan's respect for freedom of speech. In 2009, as the Democrats in Congress were moving forward with the health care proposal that would come to be known as *Obamacare*, Americans voiced strong opposition to the bill. In a blatant attempt to curtail free speech and clamp down on negative discussions about the proposal, Obama's White House set up an email address where American citizens could report on their neighbors and other fellow citizens. The snitch email system resembled totalitarian regimes' citizen spying techniques.

The White House described the new initiative with an alarming blog post: "There is a lot of disinformation about health insurance reform out there, spanning from control of personal finances to end of life care. These rumors often travel just below the surface via chain emails or through casual conversation. Since we can't keep track of all of them here at the White House, we're asking for your help. If you get an email or see something on the web about health insurance reform that seems fishy, send it to flag@whitehouse.gov." The Obama administration failed to explain how it could possibly be the responsibility of the federal government to "keep track" of what Americans were saying about the proposed law.

In the end, after Republicans in Congress exposed the totalitarian nature of Obama's attempted database of Americans' comments, the Obama White House abandoned the project.

Citizens United

A pivotal moment for freedom of speech occurred in 2010, when Citizens United, a conservative advocacy organization, won a monumental Supreme Court case.

The 2002 campaign finance reform known as McCain-Feingold, which, among other things, sought to limit federal contributions to campaigns, had a chilling effect on political speech as soon as it was signed into law. In 2008, Citizens United wanted to advertise and distribute a documentary film, *Hillary: The Movie*. Under McCain-Feingold, the distribution of the film was interpreted as a form of electioneering communications, and constituted a criminal act, allowing for prosecution and even jail time for engaging in constitutionally protected free speech.

Citizens United sued the federal government on the grounds that silencing free speech was a violation of the First Amendment. The Supreme Court agreed, and the Citizens United case protected political free speech.

During the first oral arguments in that case, lawyers for the federal government revealed just how much McCain-Feingold allowed the government to clamp down on free speech. In a telling exchange, Chief Justice John Roberts asked the solicitor general if, under McCain-Feingold, certain books could be banned. Roberts presented a hypothetic book: "It's a 500-page book, and at the end it says, 'and so vote for X!' The government could ban that?"[9] The solicitor general, without hesitation, confirmed

McCain-Feingold had empowered the government not only to ban that book, but to imprison the author.

Progressives today promise to work to overturn *Citizens United*, but Americans should remember the oral arguments in the case. It is a slippery slope once the federal government criminalizes certain speech. The solicitor general could easily imagine a scenario in America in which authors would be thrown into prison and books could be banned by the federal government. This bleak possibility should serve as a timeless warning against the progressives' plans. Put in plain English: the federal government—the executive branch—has gone too far. Prison time was meant for bank robbers, not for people exercising their right to free speech. Put drug dealers away? Sure. But those in violation of McCain-Feingold?

It's a step too far.

Freedom of Speech in the Age of the Internet

The internet is an area where the Obama Administration accelerated the growth and reach of the federal government. In 2015, Obama's Federal Communications Commission implemented a series of regulations for the internet, called "net neutrality." Those regulations, which mandate how providers offer internet services, had the effect of reducing innovation and investment by stifling the natural flow of competition, thus reducing the number of people with access to broadband and interfering with free speech.

In 2017, President Trump nominated Ajit Pai to the FCC, and Pai promised to roll back the damaging regulations implemented under Obama. Later that year, with Pai on board, the FCC voted to reverse net neutrality, which ushered in a new age of internet freedom, with more Americans gaining access to the broadband internet.

The FCC produced a report in the summer of 2019, on broadband usage across the country, which revealed the devastating consequences of the Obama regulations, and the immediate positive effects of repealing net neutrality.[10] At the time of the report, internet speeds in the United States were at an all-time high, up nearly 40 percent. Many people might assume progress and growth in internet usage and access have steadily increased year after year since the 1990s. The report, however, tells a disturbing tale about how nearly five million fewer Americans had access to broadband internet from 2016 to 2017, from 26.1 million to 21.3 million, all thanks to onerous government regulations. Those regulations stifled broadband access in rural areas and made internet access more expensive, and even unattainable, in certain parts of the country.

The contrast between progressives and conservatives in their approach to the internet boils down to the clash between control and competition. The progressives believe the answer is to create more regulations and shield Americans from market forces, while conservatives believe in the power of the free market and robust competition to foster greater opportunities and access at lower prices for more Americans. Net neutrality was always about one thing—greater government control of the internet. By taking on the power to regulate the internet for fairness, the FCC was paving the way for scenarios in which the federal government would be able to determine what constituted fair content, police free speech, tax internet usage, monitor conversations and content on the web, and shut down certain internet providers.

Progressives Attack Free Speech

Progressives today use a variety of techniques to attack freedom of speech. Because Americans, by and large, are such strident defenders of the First Amendment's robust protections of speech, progressives have had to resort to misleading attacks on free speech. One such method is to label speech they dislike as dehumanizing. This tactic is particularly common on college campuses.

Progressives frequently label speech a form of violence and claim their basic humanity is being erased by words with which they disagree. To listen to progressives' complaints today, one gets the impression the most severe forms of violence in America are a result of the First Amendment.

To take but one example, campus activists across the country have engaged in a coordinated effort to block conservative speakers from delivering speeches at their universities that might challenge the progressive narrative. These speakers are vilified as dehumanizing progressives because they call into question some of the absurdities progressives demand we accept at face value.

Progressive ideas cover a broad range of absurdities. Consider some of the progressive gems they demand we not only accept, but that we actually rearrange society to accommodate ideas rooted in fantasy: Men can get pregnant. Climate change is dramatically increasing the temperature of the earth to such an extent the earth will no longer exist within a few generations, or twelve years, as one freshman congresswoman told us. Guns never save lives, and law-abiding citizens cannot be trusted with firearms. Killing a baby who has been born and is breathing on her own is not murder; it is simply a late-term abortion.

These progressive so-called facts are pure fiction. But to challenge the progressives' ideas is, according to their narrative, to engage in violence against them, robbing them of their basic right to exist.

Progressives' main objective in shutting down free speech is to cut off the debate surrounding their ideas. Imagine if the founders took the same approach to stifle opposing views. There would have been no debate between the federalists and anti-federalists, and no discussion about the amendments we honor as the Bill of Rights.

Academic Freedom

In response to the progressives' crackdown on free speech on college campuses, the University of Chicago developed a statement on freedom of expression, which numerous other universities across the country have adopted. Since 2014, the university has mailed incoming first-year students a letter about academic freedom and freedom of expression. The letter to the Class of 2020 read, in part: "You will find that we expect members of our community to be engaged in rigorous debate, discussion, and even disagreement. At times this may challenge you and even cause discomfort. Our commitment to academic freedom means that we do not support so-called 'trigger warnings,' we do not cancel invited speakers because their topics might prove controversial, and we do not condone the creation of intellectual 'safe spaces' where individuals can retreat from ideas and perspectives at odds with their own. Fostering the free exchange of ideas reinforces a related University priority—building a campus that welcomes people of all backgrounds."[11]

These principles are referred to as The Chicago Statement. While some universities, including Princeton, Columbia, and Brown University, have adopted the statement, most of the nation's universities have doubled down on their cultures of silencing free speech in the name of creating intellectual "safe spaces."

I've heard many complaints from constituents who wonder why the federal government continues to provide hundreds of millions of dollars in funding to public and private universities. Why, they ask, is Congress propping up universities who are indoctrinating students in the politics of hate, encouraging students to shout down what they don't want to hear, who fan the flames of liberal extremism, which seeks to control what we think and say.

Universities are supposed to be open forums in the promotion of critical thinking, not in creating liberals critical of thinking. Things have gotten so out of hand President Trump stepped in, recently issuing an executive order intended to protect freedom of speech on campuses across the country.

"If a college or university does not allow you to speak, we will not give them money," Trump said, in unveiling the executive order. "It's that simple."

Freedom of the Press: The Great Bulwark of Liberty

Closely related to freedom of speech is another pillar of our liberty as Americans: the freedom of the press. In drafting the Bill of Rights, Madison called freedom of the press "one of the great bulwarks of liberty."[12] In another instance, Madison argued, in an opinion editorial for the *National Gazette,* he argued the "circulation of newspapers through the entire body of the people" fosters rigorous debate among the people about the important issues of the day.[13]

There are two equally important aspects of freedom of the press. On the one hand, there must be respect for freedom of the press. But on the other hand, the press must also respect its vital role in holding government accountable.

For the founders, freedom of the press was the foundation for a free society. Jefferson noted, "the only security of all is in a free press."[14] While serving as U.S. minister to France, he went even further in stating the importance of the free press, writing: "Were it left to me to decide whether we should have a government without newspapers, or newspapers without a government, I should not hesitate a moment to prefer the latter."[15]

One of the threats to the esteem Americans have for the press is a self-inflicted wound by members of the media. Fake news, which has existed since before our founding, has become more pervasive. Reporters at major publications frequently distort the truth or make up their own news to corroborate the far-left narrative of certain events. The Kavanaugh case comes to mind. The result is journalistic standards and ethics are compromised. But even worse, the respect for the institution of freedom of the press is tarnished as well.

Jefferson struggled with fake news in his day, too. Surveying the falsified stories in the newspaper then, he lamented, "Nothing can now be believed which is seen in a newspaper. Truth itself becomes suspicious by being put into that polluted vehicle."[16]

The worst consequence of fake news is Americans have lost faith in the press to provide accountability and oversight over the government.

I sympathize with Jefferson. Back in 2018, I watched in deep dismay as the Denver Post ran multiple stories noting a gubernatorial candidate's great-great-grandfather was allegedly part of the KKK. Why, I wondered, was this candidate, a statewide officeholder, being punished for the sins—not even verified—of a distant relative? But that's what the progressives do—divide us.

Tension with the Press

While touring the Capitol, I always pause on the east staircase of the House wing to ask my guests if they see the reddish-brown spots on the steps. Occasionally, someone will say, "Is that blood?"

Indeed, those are blood stains on the stairs, a reminder of a gun fight in 1890, between a former congressman and a reporter. Charles Kincaid, a newspaper reporter, wrote an article in 1887, suggesting then Congressman William Taulbee of Kentucky was engaged in an extramarital affair. The article sparked a years-long feud between the two.

Although Taulbee chose not to run again after the story was published, his new job as a lobbyist required him to walk the halls of Congress. Over the years, he and Kincaid would run into each other on the Hill, with an increasing amount of vitriol in their exchanges. One particularly sharp argument prompted Taulbee to warn the reporter to arm himself. Kincaid took the threat seriously, returned to the Capitol with a gun, and shot the former congressman, who died two weeks later from the wound.

Those blood stains serve as a reminder of the tensions between politicians and the press. I also tell my guests a jury acquitted Kincaid—further proving Congress was every bit as popular in 1890 as it is today.

John Adams and the Alien and Sedition Acts of 1798

John Adams held a troubling view of the press, and his administration used the pretext of a possible war with France as an excuse to crack down on the media. The federalists in charge of the government in the 1790s, passed the Alien and Sedition Acts, which the Adams administration used to target his opponents, seeking to jail anyone who would "write, print, utter or publish" anything opposing President Adams, his administration, or Congress.

Jefferson and Madison saw the tyrannical roots of the Alien and Sedition Acts, and they penned their opposition anonymously in two documents known as the Kentucky and Virginia Resolutions. Those resolutions argued the Alien and Sedition Acts were unconstitutional.

Jefferson's Kentucky Resolution identified the acts as "nothing short of despotism" and argued the laws were "palpable violations of the said constitution."[17]

Madison, the author of the Virginia Resolution, gave an even more biting analysis. The Sedition Act "exercises in like manner, a power not delegated by the Constitution...which more than any other, ought to produce universal alarm, because it is levelled against the right of freely examining public characters and measures, and of free communication among the people thereon, which has ever been justly deemed, the only effectual guardian of every other right."

The freedom of the press and the closely related freedom of speech remain today the guardians of every other right we enjoy. Without that free flow of communication among the people, as Madison noted, the government is free to implement the most tyrannical measures.

The criticisms Madison and Jefferson raised were more than theoretical concerns. The federal government convicted more than two dozen people under the onerous act. One publisher, and even a member of Congress (Matthew Lyon from Vermont), served time in jail for daring to criticize President Adams. In an indication of the unpopularity of the Sedition Act, Lyon won re-election from jail.

The *Philadelphia Aurora*, a paper supportive of Jefferson's party, argued in its October 14, 1800 issue, that a Jefferson victory on election day would help usher in "the liberty of the press."[18] President Adams, it should be noted, attempted to charge the printer of that paper, William Duane, on sedition. The editors' wager on whether Americans' disliked Adams' crackdown on the press proved correct; Jefferson won the presidency on the promise of restoring freedom of the press.

Wilson Resorts to Censorship and Propaganda

Almost 120 years after the Alien and Sedition Act, another U.S. president, Woodrow Wilson, employed similar tactics against the free press. President

Wilson viewed the press as an organ of the federal government, and in a 1917 letter to the chairman of the House judiciary committee, wrote that he sought "authority to exercise censorship over the Press."[19] He frequently cited "public safety" concerns as the justification for his efforts.

Once Congress declared war in 1917, officially bringing the United States into the first World War, Wilson issued an executive order to create a propaganda committee, known as the Committee on Public Information.

Wilson used the world war as the backdrop to build the case that his presidency's objective was to "make the world safe for democracy"— language recognizable today for its seductive promise of security. In his quest to make the world safe, Wilson justified curtailing press freedom. In the name of security, Wilson devised a plan to control and censor news coverage.

In 1917, Congress passed the Espionage Act, which Wilson and his supporters said would stop interference with military recruitment, and protect the United States from enemies during wartime.

The following year, Congress passed a series of amendments to the Espionage Act, known as the Sedition Act of 1918. These amendments to the Espionage Act made it a federal crime to use "disloyal, profane, scurrilous, or abusive language" about the Constitution, the government, or the American flag.

In delivering a wartime speech, President Wilson explained his rationale for supporting these acts. "If there should be disloyalty, it will be dealt with a firm hand of repression," he said. Even Wilson knew he was institutionalizing repressive measures.

Thousands of people were charged under the Espionage Act. One individual, Jacob Abrams, sued the federal government after he was charged with espionage. He and five others were convicted for distributing leaflets from the windows of a building in New York City. One of the leaflets criticized the use of American troops in the global war and denounced sending troops to Russia. The leaflet encouraged Americans to advocate for the government to discontinue producing weapons to use against Russia. A second pamphlet called out the United States for being a barrier to the Russian Revolution.

The charge against the pamphleteers was they were inciting resistance to Wilson's war effort, and they received ten to twenty years in prison. The

Supreme Court upheld their conviction in a seven-to-two ruling, finding the defendants' freedom of speech had not been violated.

One of the two dissenters was Justice Oliver Wendell Holmes, who wrote in the dissenting opinion that it is tempting for governments to crack down on opposing views and to use the law to "sweep away all opposition."[20] But he argued, a far better way for those ideas to be halted is through the "free trade in ideas," where "the best test of truth is the power of the thought to get itself accepted in the competition of the market, and that truth is the only ground upon which their wishes safely can be carried out."[21]

Holmes was among the first to describe in such clear language a marketplace of ideas, with competition and rational individuals empowered to make decisions about the merits of one idea over another.

Nixon's War with the Press

Richard Nixon, who served in the White House some sixty years later, picked up where Wilson left off in the war against the press. Nixon compiled a list of press "enemies," and used the IRS to audit his political opponents. His surrogates even mounted a campaign to yank the license of a television station owned by *The Washington Post*, the paper whose investigative reporters were a constant thorn in Nixon's side.

The Nixon administration engaged in other ruthless tactics against reporters. Journalists' phone lines were tapped. The Nixon administration authorized the IRS to investigate tax returns by prominent journalists critical of Nixon. He, of course, could look back at FDR's abuse of the IRS to find a template for how the IRS could be used as a weapon to intimidate opponents.

More recently, President Obama struggled with the First Amendment throughout his time at the White House. His Department of Justice, perhaps inspired by Nixon's tapping of journalists' phone lines, made the frightening move of monitoring the phone records of journalists Obama deemed hostile to his agenda. The Justice Department showed little regard for the confidentiality of journalists' sources when it attempted to compel a *New York Times* reporter to release the name of one such source.

In another Nixon-like move, the Obama White House adopted the language of enmity toward news reports. Obama's communications director, Anita Dunn, said the White House had adopted a new policy toward Fox News: "We're going to treat them the way we would treat an opponent."[22]

The list of Obama's offenses against the press is long. His administration relentlessly prosecuted leakers and whistleblowers, and secretly surveilled the private phone records of nearly one hundred Associated Press reporters.

The Obama administration was following the Wilson/Nixon playbook down to an intricate detail, from creating enemy lists with journalists' names to eroding transparency for the press.

Fireside Tweets

President Donald Trump has had an adversarial relationship with the press from the start. He has received a level of scrutiny and hostility from the media no other president has ever had to endure. Trump's favorite medium for communication is his Twitter account, which he uses as his press office at times and in lieu of press releases or press conferences. His Twitter feed is where he has announced major trade policies, as well as White House staff changes.

Trump's preference for tweets in dealing with hostile members of the press has a long history. Franklin Delano Roosevelt perfected the art of direct communication with Americans through his popular fireside chats—the evening radio broadcasts from the White House between 1933 and 1944. Similarly, President Kennedy used television, without the constraints of a formal press conference, to directly reach Americans.

Trump's frustration with the press is nothing new. In fact, Lyndon B. Johnson was often upset with the media's unfair treatment of his presidency. He once quipped, "If one morning I walked on top of the water across the Potomac River, the headline that afternoon would read: 'President Can't Swim.'"

The Free Flow of Communication

Progressives today are using the same tricks as employed in previous periods in American history, drawing heavily from Wilson, Nixon, and Obama. As

Justice Holmes pointed out in his dissenting opinion, the proper place for thoughts to thrive or die is in the free market of ideas. Unpopular or rotten ideas will not withstand the rigorous testing and challenges of free people engaged in dialogue in our society, and will be stamped out that way.

Holmes went on to write, we as Americans, should be "eternally vigilant against attempts to check the expression of opinions that we loathe,"[23] even in the name of security. Progressives are fond of shouting down, silencing, or using the power of the government to choke out opposing views. They often do so in their pursuit of "greater security," whether that security is in the form of economic security, or "climate security," or so-called "safe spaces" for intellectual security.

The reality is progressives' ideas and worldviews often fall flat with the American public. It is no wonder, then, they are so quick to employ the same tyrannical and silencing tactics our founders wanted to avoid. Madison, the primary author of the Constitution, understood the ideal government was a representative republic, not a pure democracy, to shield us from the inflammatory rhetoric of mob rule. He wanted to avoid what he called the "mischief of factions," which would confuse issues of public policy, and he wanted to create a system in which enlightened delegates, selected by the people, would guide our great nation.

We've moved far from that aspiration. Indeed, the founders would be shocked by the state of affairs, how progressives are trying to hijack our right to free speech. Franklin, in particular, would find the goal of the freedom of speech he so fervently talked about subverted by progressives today.

CHAPTER 8

Religious Freedom

"Let the pulpit resound with the doctrines and sentiments
of religious liberty."[1]

—JOHN ADAMS

John Peter Gabriel Muhlenberg isn't a household name, but it ought to be. As a youngster, he ran away from school before he found his way, becoming an ordained minister. Well-schooled in theology, he took to the pulpit in Woodstock, Virginia, one memorable day, January 21, 1776, and delivered a sermon that still rings in American legend.

Opening to the third chapter of Ecclesiastes, the reverend recited the familiar verse, "There is a time for everything." When he reached the eighth verse, he intoned there is "a time for war and a time for peace." And this, he said, was indeed a time for war.

According to lore, he proceeded to discard his clerical robe, under which he wore a Continental Army colonel's uniform. The man of the cloth was becoming a man of war, joining the rebels in the American Revolution. In the moment, he exhorted members of his congregation to join him in the cause, and 162 men did just that.

You can almost hear his exhortation, the way his statue stands boldly in the crypt in the Capitol building, shown just as he's throwing off his pastor's robe, revealing his military garb.

There is something epic in the way Muhlenberg's image soars high above ground, a grand figure reminiscent of a pastor in the pulpit, as we, in the congregation, peer up in honorific attention.

As it happened, his brother, Frederick Augustus Muhlenberg, was also a minister, at a New York City church, and, like their father, he didn't approve of John Peter Gabriel's entry into military service.

But then the British bombarded and invaded New York and torched Frederick Augustus's church to the ground before his own eyes. Frederick August and his family were forced to flee. The harrowing experience was enough to prompt him to get involved, becoming a delegate to the Continental Congress in 1779. Later, elected to Congress, Frederick Augustus became the first speaker of the U.S. House of Representatives.

So let it be known, ours was a great nation built on the foundation of great men of faith.

Speaking of which, there is a direct link between John Peter Gabriel Muhlenberg and the man who personally appealed to him to join the military campaign for freedom—General George Washington, the ultimate soldier. Both were strong men of deep faith; Washington is credited as saying, "We need chaplains," in response to the spiritual needs of his soldiers. Thus, he established the Army Chaplain Corps, further entwining our history with fidelity to faith.

The echoes of our religious foundation in freedom can be felt throughout the Capitol. It was Benjamin Franklin, an elder statesman at the Constitutional Convention, who counseled the assembled by saying, "I have lived a long time, sir, a long time, and the longer I live, the more convincing proofs I see of this truth—that God governs in the affairs of men."

And it was Founding Father Thomas Jefferson who wrote the Virginia Statute for Religious Freedom, which became the template and model for the First Amendment to the Constitution's protections of religious liberty. Listen to the inextricable link to our religious foundation:

> *"Almighty God hath created the mind free.... All attempts to influence it by temporal punishments or burdens...are a departure from the plan of the Holy Author of our religion.... No man shall be compelled to frequent or support any religious worship or ministry or shall otherwise suffer on account of his religious opinions of belief, but all men shall be free to profess, and by argument to maintain, their opinions in matters of religion."*[2]

Even more familiar perhaps is what Jefferson made indelible in the Declaration of Independence, that "We hold these truths to be self-evident, that all men are created equal, that they are endowed by their creator with certain unalienable rights, that among these are life, liberty, and the pursuit of happiness."

Notice the emphasis that these are God-given rights. Our founders were Christians of abiding belief, who were certain there were things God wanted when humans were placed on this earth. Our rights were God-given, not government-given; because if government gave us our rights, government could take our rights away just as easily. But government can't. We are endowed by God with "unalienable" rights.

When I take visitors to the House chapel, opening the door with a special code, they are witnesses to our religious freedoms in action. Constituents on the tour are taken aback. They are surprised there is a chapel within the U.S. Capitol. They don't know chaplains have honored space in the Capitol as well. They don't realize there is a church service in the rotunda every Wednesday evening. The left has hammered away at those who would display faith in public life. And yet it's everywhere in the Capitol, steeped in our intricate history.

Into the rotunda I take my visitors. That's where I point to the inside of the dome and show angels carrying George Washington's spirit to Heaven, as rendered in the famous painting, *The Apotheosis of Washington.* The Christian fresco—one of the most prominent religious symbols in the Capitol—floats 180 feet above the Rotunda, under which resides the crypt where Washington's body was laid to rest in state until his wife chose for her husband to be interred on the grounds of his home in Mt. Vernon.

One visitor asks, "What about the separation of church and state?"

My response: "Never heard of that."

Nods emerge from the group. No one need be a member of Congress to get it. This is as it should be—the inextricable link between our founding on a strong foundation of faith and who we are as a people. It's what makes us great. There's a sense of confirmation murmuring among the constituents; they didn't expect what they saw on this tour—so many symbols of faith, of religion—but they begin to take it in, the power and the glory.

* * *

We take for granted the oft-stated term, "separation of church and state," but the origins of the phrase tell us about who we are, where we came from, and how the left has sought to distort the truth.

In 1802, Jefferson wrote a letter to the Danbury Baptist Association in Connecticut, in which he said, "Believing with you that religion is a matter which lies solely between Man & his God, that he owes account to none other for his faith or his worship, that the legitimate powers of government reach actions only, and not opinions, I contemplate with sovereign reverence that act of the whole American people which declared that their legislature should 'make no law respecting an establishment of religion, or prohibiting the free exercise thereof,' thus building a wall of separation between Church & State."[3]

In his missive, Jefferson was hailing religious freedom, carved out of the wilderness of our new nation.

Jefferson couldn't have been clearer when he asked, "Can the liberties of a nation be secure when we have removed a conviction that these liberties are the gift of God?"[4]

Our founding fathers, in walling off the state from interfering with the church, were celebrating the free exercise of religion. They were not anti-religion; far from it. They were paving the way for America to be the greatest beacon of religious freedom in the world.

We gain insight into the importance of religious freedom, given where the founders placed it within the Bill of Rights, near the freedom of the press and freedom of speech. The first part of the First Amendment states,

"Congress shall make no law respecting an establishment of religion or prohibiting the free exercise" of our faith.

The two-pronged idea is clear: First, we have the freedom from being forced to follow a certain religion, or being compelled, as many people still are today in other countries, to pay a tax to support the state-sanctioned church. Second, we have the liberty to practice any religion we want—or no religion at all—and to live our lives in accordance with our faith.

But the meaning of Jefferson's letter was distorted by none other than the Supreme Court, in yet another display of legislating from the bench. Not long after the era of the Marshall court, which expanded the Supreme Court's power and domain, the high court did it again in 1878, when it issued its first opinion to address the First Amendment's protection of religious liberties.

The court, examining Jefferson's letter, ruled the government could intervene in the religious affairs of man. The court upheld the conviction of a man who unsuccessfully argued that as a Mormon it was his free exercise of religion to practice polygamy. In Reynolds v. United States, the court stated the First Amendment deprived Congress "of all legislative power over mere opinion but was left free to reach actions which were in violation of social duties or subversive of good order." The court continued by saying, "Can a man excuse his [illegal] practices…because of his religious belief? To permit this would be to make the professed doctrines of religious belief superior to the law of the land, and in effect to permit every citizen to become a law unto himself."[5]

One of the principles behind that ruling was a distortion of Jefferson's meaning. He was saying the state must be separated from the church to ensure the state doesn't impinge on our religious freedoms. He wasn't saying, as the court deemed, that the state must be separate from the church to ensure churches don't have influence on the affairs of man. But the court's broad language in Reynolds opened the door for Congress to legislate in violation of an individual's religious practices.

Not surprisingly, the progressives of today have also quoted liberally from the Jefferson letter, continuing to distort its meaning for their own ends—moving us away from our faith, in favor of the expansion of big government to control our lives and liberty.

* * *

A plaque sits on my double-pedestal, standard-issue wooden desk in the Rayburn House Office Building. It reads: "Pray."

For a time, the plaque faced the visitors being seated in my office. But then one day, it occurred to me, I should flip it around to face me as a reminder to pray myself. Which I do. I will ask my staff to leave me alone for a moment before I head to the floor of the House, before I give a speech, before I go to a committee meeting to ask questions. Sitting at my desk, I pray.

In prayer, I reflect on our heritage, as framed in an image on the wall next to my desk: of George Washington at Valley Forge, hands clasped, on bended knee, by his trusty white horse, praying to God.

I'm reminded of one of my other American heroes, Abraham Lincoln, who was often seen from the back, on his knees, praying sometimes for hours at a stretch, and people were warded off, not to go anywhere near the president in those quiet moments with God.

Lincoln signed into law a proclamation recognizing a National Fast Day to focus the nation's attention on praying. The proclamation read, in part, "It behooves us, then, to humble ourselves before the offended Power, to confess national sins, and to pray for clemency and forgiveness."[6]

It's a sentiment largely lost in the harangues of the left, who would have us believe we can't talk in the public sphere about faith in and reliance on God. They slam the door on any whiff of religion, as a violation of the separation of church and state.

It isn't.

What progressives are doing is upholding another belief system: Marxism. Let's not forget Karl Marx called for the abolition of religion. Religion, he understood, gave people hope in something outside the communist agenda, and an identity through God, rather than through their work and with other workers. Religion, for those very reasons, continues to be a barrier to the progressives' agenda today.

The influence of Marx—and the negation of religion—continues to prevail in the progressives' onslaught on our religious freedoms, in their attempt to create bigger government, to control what we do, how we think, what we are to believe—or not believe.

Take, for example, the Johnson Amendment. Back in the 1950s, Then U.S. Senator Lyndon B. Johnson of Texas, didn't take kindly to criticism coming from the pulpit and elsewhere. In particular, two nonprofit groups were campaigning against him, calling him a "closet Communist." So in his typical heavy-handed fashion, he proposed a provision to the U.S. tax code, in 1954, prohibiting all 501(c)(3) nonprofit organizations from endorsing or opposing political candidates, at the risk of losing their nonprofit status.

It was controversial back then, and still is. The Johnson Amendment serves as a powerful deterrent—some call it a form a censorship—stopping religious leaders from exercising their freedom of expression.

Obama, another progressive after LBJ, did his fair share to erode our religious freedoms.

In recent years, and especially during Obama's presidency, we started to hear him talk about the "freedom to worship." That, if you're not paying close attention, is a liberal creation skirting our constitutional right to freedom of religion. Freedom of worship is a narrow freedom meaning people are free to worship in a church or synagogue or other place of worship. It leaves out one of the most significant—and beautiful—aspects of the life of a believer, and that is the ability to live out our faith in our daily lives.

Another assault on our religious freedoms came from Obama's sweeping healthcare law, Obamacare.

It called for a government mandate that all healthcare insurers cover twenty varieties of FDA-approved contraceptives, at no cost to patients. It didn't matter what your beliefs were, whether birth control flew in the face of your religious beliefs.

In 2012, Hobby Lobby, a chain of arts and crafts stores owned by David Green and his evangelical Christian family, filed suit against the federal government, arguing that requiring the company to cover certain abortion-inducing drugs, such as the morning-after pill, violated the family's religious beliefs, which "forbid them from participating in, providing access to, paying for, training others to engage in, or otherwise supporting abortion-causing drugs and devices."

The Green family, like many Americans, believe life begins at conception, and abortifacients constitute a form of abortion. What's more, the Greens believed the government should not compel individuals or companies to provide contraceptives that conflict with their religious beliefs; it is, they argued, a private decision.

Hobby Lobby cited the First Amendment to the Constitution to protect their religious beliefs. About two years later, in a landmark decision, the Supreme Court ruled in Hobby Lobby's favor. While the high court did not weigh in on Hobby Lobby's claims under the First Amendment, it was the first time the high court recognized a for-profit company's assertion of their rights to exercise their religious beliefs. The Supreme Court made its ruling based on the provisions of the Religious Freedom Restoration Act. Enacted by Congress in 1993, it required laws restricting religious practice must show they serve a compelling need. The contentious, split ruling of *Burwell v. Hobby Lobby* allowed small, closely held companies the right to decline to provide contraceptive benefits on their healthcare plans, as mandated by Obamacare, on the grounds of protecting their owners' religious liberty.

A year later, in 2015, the high court took on a similar case involving the Little Sisters of the Poor, a group of nuns who run a Roman Catholic order with dozens of homes for the low-income elderly in the United States. The nuns said Obamacare violated their beliefs with its requirement to cover contraceptive devices. It was, they said, a sin under Roman Catholic doctrine.

The Little Sisters won their big case, averting a government-imposed fine of $70 million. But in an unfortunate epilogue to the Little Sister's fight, two states—California and Pennsylvania—have sought to compel the courts to take away the nuns' religious exemption, forcing them to comply with Obamacare's mandate of contraceptive coverage, or be fined tens of millions of dollars.

"What it all adds up to is a fight on political and ideological grounds," the Little Sisters said, in a statement on their website.[7]

They never wanted this fight, the nuns said. All they ask for is the ability to practice their constitutional freedom of religion and "get back to caring for the elderly in need."

The assaults have nonetheless continued from the left, as witnessed when the Supreme Court agreed in 2017 to take on the case of Jack Phillips, the owner of Masterpiece Cakeshop, a bakery in Lakewood, Colorado.

About five years earlier, in 2012, a gay couple, Charlie Craig and David Mullins, were planning to be legally married in Massachusetts with a celebration back in Colorado, with family and friends. When they ordered a custom wedding cake, Phillips, a Christian, declined, citing his religious beliefs. The Supreme Court would go on to rule in 2015 the Constitution guaranteed a right to same-sex marriage. The baker told the couple they could order other baked goods; he even agreed to make the gay couple a birthday cake, but not a wedding cake. Making a wedding cake, the baker felt, was tantamount to participating in their wedding itself, which would force him to do something affirmatively in violation of his religious beliefs.

The gay couple didn't discuss it further with the baker, but filed a complaint with the Colorado Civil Rights Commission, against Phillips. The commission ruled the baker discriminated against the gay couple, and when other local courts upheld the commission's determination, the baker took his case to the Supreme Court.

Ultimately, the high court ruled the state commission violated the baker's rights, reversing the agency's decision. Writing for the majority, Justice Anthony Kennedy said the commission's review of Phillips' case showed hostility toward the baker's religious views when the commission compared his assertions to the defense of the Holocaust or slavery. Kennedy also cautioned, "these disputes must be resolved with tolerance, without undue disrespect to sincere religious beliefs…."

Kennedy's caution hasn't been heeded. Invasions of our religious freedom keep cropping up. In one of the latest examples, a Christian couple in Minnesota, who operate a business offering wedding videography, fought for their religious beliefs—and freedom of speech—when they were threatened with violating the law for not agreeing to create films celebrating same-sex marriage.

Carl and Angel Larsen, who run a Christian videography business, Telescope Media Group, said making videos celebrating a same-sex marriage would violate their religious beliefs; marriage they said, is a lifelong institution between one man and one woman. They said they sought to fight against a "powerful cultural narrative undermining the historic, biblically orthodox definition of marriage as between one man and one woman."

As a result, the Larsens filed a federal suit, asserting that by adhering to their religious belief, it would place them in violation of the state's public accommodation laws, leaving them in jeopardy of heavy fines, or even jail time.

In the summer of 2019, the 8th U.S. Circuit Court of Appeals ruled the couple could pursue their legal challenge. "Because the First Amendment allows the Larsens to choose when to speak and what to say, we reverse the dismissal of two of their claims," the appeals court ruled.[8]

Nonetheless, incursions on our religious freedoms continue to manifest themselves across the political spectrum. Notice, for instance, how confirmation battles in the Senate often center on grilling federal candidates over their religious beliefs, including Catholic nominees who have expressed opposition to same-sex marriage or abortion.

Speaking of officeholders, it's worth noting when, say, the House Judiciary Committee is called to order, witnesses are sworn in and they take an oath—"so help you, God." And yet what we know of God—as revealed in the Bible—has been so far removed from our lives by progressives, the greatest book in history is an afterthought, or even less. The religion of the left—secularism—seeks to discredit morality, disregard the afterlife, and undermine the meaning of families, leaving so many bound to the state.

We have Obama, among others, to thank for rejecting our religious freedoms. When he was president, it came out in 2009, that the White House ordered Georgetown University to cover all religious symbols where he was scheduled to make a speech at the Jesuit university. Imagine that. Covering the cross—a symbol of Jesus Christ, who stands for only goodness and greatness.

As if that wasn't offensive enough, Obama tried to erode other aspects of our religious foundation during his tenure in the White House. The Hyde Amendment, for instance, was supposed to curb the use of federal funds to pay for abortions, except in exceptional cases, such as to save the life of the woman. Obama assured the American people he respected the Hyde Amendment, that there would be no attempt to circumvent it. But of course, that wasn't the case. Planned Parenthood, the leading abortion provider, receives hundreds of millions of dollars in government grants. They say it's for overhead costs, not abortions. I call it clever accounting.

What's equally clever is how Planned Parenthood obfuscates its ignominious origins.

In 1921, Margaret Sanger established the American Birth Control League, the forerunner of Planned Parenthood. Sanger is held up as a paragon of virtue among abortion rights activists. What they don't like to mention, or don't want to acknowledge, is Sanger was closely associated with Lothrop Stoddard, a member of the Ku Klux Klan and a Nazi sympathizer. What's more, Sanger promoted what is politely called eugenics, which is another way of saying she believed in eliminating the reproduction of those in society who were considered "unfit." Sanger was associated with an initiative called the *Negro Project*, aimed at delivering birth control to poor black people. In a letter, Sanger wrote, "We do not want word to go out that we want to exterminate the Negro population,"[9] which some have interpreted to mean she meant to forcibly reduce the black population.

This reminds me of the time I had the pleasure to question Candace Owens, a black activist, in the House Judiciary Committee, in 2019. I clearly heard her deep concern about the impact abortion is having on the black community. Candace has written that "62% percent of all abortions in Alabama are performed on black women. Black women account for only 7 percent of the population but make up roughly 40% of the abortions performed in America. Due to abortion, the black population growth has completely stagnated—we are the ONLY race population that is not growing. Planned Parenthood was founded by an avowed racist who said her aim was to exterminate black people like weeds. Planned Parenthood clinics are strategically placed in black neighborhoods. Abortion is not only murder, but it is a silent black genocide that has been mainstreamed by racist liberals...."[10]

* * *

The sad truth is the constancy of the withering attacks from the left on our religious freedoms and foundation. Prayer has been banished from schools, while crosses are removed from public spheres.

Jesus called on us to love our neighbors. That's a call for us, as individuals, churches, and others to act as the Good Samaritan did, coming to the aid of another, including one who is different than ourselves. The progressives, though, would forgo the lesson altogether and place the responsibility in the hands of the government to solve our problems, to serve as the primary provider of charity, whether through the failed modern welfare system or the massive progressive programs FDR plunked down on America.

Whatever happened to the bedrock of our nation—family, church, community? The left has been all too effective in removing us from our reliance on faith, separating us from our religious foundation. Progressives have erected a secular, state-sanctioned religion, enforced by extreme political correctness about the words we are permitted to use, to the point of erasing our history and heritage.

The founders of our nation recognized religion and the public expression of faith as pillars in society. Writing in the mid-1800s, the Frenchman Alexis de Tocqueville marveled at the influence of the Christian faith in society. "There is no country in the world where the Christian religion retains a greater influence over the souls of men than in America," he said, "and there can be no greater proof of its utility and its conformity to human nature than that its influence is powerfully felt over the most enlightened and free nation on earth."[11]

Regrettably, that's often no longer the case. I'm reminded of the Reverend Martin Luther King, Jr., who once cautioned, "If the church does not recapture its prophetic zeal, it will become an irrelevant social club without moral or spiritual authority."[12]

* * *

Lest it be overlooked, the words "In God We Trust" reside over the House and Senate chambers.

You can't miss the powerful phrase when it sits right above the president's head as he gives his annual State of the Union Address.

Another reminder of our great nation built on God arrives every day when the House chamber opens with a prayer, courtesy of the House chaplain. We are a religious people, plain and simple, no matter what the progressives will have you believe.

I can attest to my own faith. I can also attest to my failings as a Christian. When I get mad at people who attack me, who say something false, I can feel my blood pressure rising. That's when I say a prayer.

I remind myself this is God's commandment: Love thy neighbor.

That neighbor might happen to be sitting next to me in committee, and with their wrongheaded ideas, they can be awfully hard to love at that moment. But I do my best.

So does Archbishop Charles J. Chaput of Philadelphia. Back in 2010, when I was running for the U.S. Senate, the prelate was the archbishop of Denver, and he asked me to stop by one of the Catholic churches in Greeley, Colorado. I was happy to oblige, though I had no idea what I'd be doing there. When the day arrived, and I settled in the second pew, the archbishop made a point of stopping to nod at me on his way up to the pulpit, where he gave his homily.

I have to admit, I was caught off guard when he mentioned there was among the congregants a martyr for the cause of life, and he referred to me by name.

"Ken Buck is not of our faith," the archbishop said, "but he is of our values."

And the archbishop proceeded to tell his congregation how we must respect our public officials who stand up for life.

After the service, on his way out, the archbishop stood outside the main doors, next to me, in his ankle-length black robe and white clerical collar, shaking people's hands.

"Hi, how are you?" he'd say. "This is my friend Ken Buck, and I want you to vote for him."

I was taken aback, thinking of the old Johnson Amendment forbidding churches from endorsing political candidates. The last thing I wanted was for the archbishop to get in trouble.

"How can you say that?" I said, in an aside.

"Inside, the IRS won't let me," he said. "But outside church, I'm a citizen."

CHAPTER 9

The Second Amendment

"The right of the citizens to keep and bear arms has justly been considered, as the palladium of the liberties of a republic; since it offers a strong moral check against the usurpation and arbitrary power of rulers; and will generally, even if these are successful in the first instance, enable the people to resist and triumph over them."[1]

—JOSEPH STORY

"Come and take it."

Although the expression did not originate in America, it is now synonymous with the Second Amendment and with the distinctly American style of holding a would-be tyrannical government in check—with an armed populace.

That expression became part of the American identity back in July 1826, when the Karankawa, Tonkawa, and Comanche tribes raided and destroyed the town of Gonzales in Northeastern Mexico. The townspeople rebuilt Gonzales, but the Comanche tribe continued to attack the area. In 1831, unable to send military troops to protect the town, the Mexican government sent a six-pound cannon to help the local residents fight off Comanche raids.

A few years later, tensions increased between Mexican authorities and the recent settlers from north of the border, referred to as Texians. In 1835, the Mexican authorities sent a corporal and five soldiers to retrieve the small cannon. After a few days of negotiations, the Texians walked the soldiers out of the town without the cannon.

On September 27, 1835, the Mexican government dispatched a hundred soldiers to Gonzales with orders to retrieve the cannon. As the troops approached Gonzales, word spread through the area, and hundreds of armed volunteers streamed into the town. The Texians fashioned a white banner with the image of a black cannon in the center and the words, "Come and take it," written under it.

The Texians attacked the encroaching Mexican troops outside of town, and after a short skirmish, the cannon fired once, two Mexican soldiers died, and the troops retreated to San Antonio de Bexar. While the events outside of Gonzales had little military significance, it united the Texians and led, two days later, to a declaration of war from Stephen Austin. Four months later, 180 Texians fought against four thousand Mexican soldiers in the Battle of the Alamo. After the battle of San Jacinto, in April 1836, Santa Anna and the Mexican Army retreated south of the Rio Grande River, and Texas became a Republic.

What history taught us: The Gonzales flag, with its defiant slogan, energized the local population to rally for Texas independence.

It shouldn't go without notice that Austin's marble statue resides in the Capitol; he stands atop a pedestal, his rifle resting against him—one of the few images here wielding a firearm.

The phrase, "Come and take it," on the Gonzales flag predated the fight for Texas independence, inspiring others to show courage and resistance in the face of tyranny. The expression traces its roots to 480 B.C., as the defiant answer of King Leonidas I to the surrender demand of Xerxes, King of Persia, at the battle of Thermopylae. Later, in November 1778, a British commander demanded the surrender of Continental army forces at Fort Morris, Georgia. In response, the continental army commander, Colonel McIntosh, wrote, "As to surrendering the fort, receive this laconic reply: COME AND TAKE IT!"[2]

For various reasons, including the bold response from Colonel McIntosh, the British forces withdrew.

Most of my tours begin in my office, in the Rayburn House Office Building. My guests gather to drop off their belongings, and I review the preliminary rules of the tour. That is, pictures are allowed everywhere but the House chambers; please thank the capitol police officer for opening the historical rooms after-hours, and be quiet when we enter office space. I also talk about the Gonzales flag I have hanging in my office.

While I am not from the Republic of Texas, nor do I represent a Texas congressional district, I share many of the same values of gun-respecting Texans. As I describe the history of the Gonzales flag, I can see heads nod in agreement as my guests understand the initial move by an aggressor is to disarm his opponent; a bully always picks a fight with the weakest individual in a group, and we, as Americans, have learned that fighting for a just cause is worth the sacrifice. Someone a lot smarter than I am once said, "The thing that sets Americans apart from all other people in the world is that they will die on their feet before they will live on their knees."

I often invite my guests into my office and show them the AR-15 semi-automatic rifle hanging on the wall. It is painted red, white, and blue. I sent a picture of the gun to my son when he was deployed with the Army. He told me it wasn't well-camouflaged, but the good news was the terrorists would know who killed them.

I offer the guests the opportunity to take their picture holding the gun, and all but a few times, my guests have jumped at the opportunity. When someone declines a picture, I know it is going to be a short tour. I don't play well with the faint of heart.

Getting an AR-15 into a congressional office is a story all by itself. A friend of mine gave me the gun after my election to Congress in 2014. I checked with the House ethics lawyers to make sure I could accept the gift. The ethics lawyers approved my receipt of the gift after a few months. Then I asked the Capitol police if I could place an AR-15 on display in my office. They weren't too happy, but they said I had the authority to have a firearm in my office. Honestly, I think they were jealous. It is a pretty cool rifle.

Then came the big test. I contacted the District of Columbia police, and they granted permission to transport the gun from the airport in Virginia to my office. The gun had to be transported in a hardened, triple-locked case, and be unloaded, of course. Then TSA provided instructions on how to get the gun on the plane from Colorado to Virginia before arriving at my Congressional office.

I got everything in writing, because my goal in Congress is to leave undefeated and unindicted. I didn't think it was a high bar until I took a picture standing next to my friend Trey Gowdy, with the red, white, and blue AR-15, and posted the picture on social media. Well, the Democrats didn't think much of the gun. Some operative called law enforcement officials in the District of Columbia and asked them, "If you knew a congressman had an AR-15 in D.C., would you investigate?" By asking that way, they got a positive response.

Next thing I knew, *The Washington Post* online edition ran a story about my gun-wielding ways.[3] I sent the written permissions I had received to *The Post*. I also told the reporter I had disabled the gun and put a trigger lock on the gun for good measure. It was a harmless museum item.

When *The Post* reporter asked me why I took those precautions, I told him it was like putting a chastity belt on a eunuch. I just wanted to make doubly sure nothing bad happened.

Since the 1960s, progressives have argued for gun control and the abolition of handgun possession. They have used various lines of reasoning to explain why we should implement fierce gun control, but each premise is easily refuted. As a member of the House Judiciary Committee, I have enjoyed exposing the progressives' flimsy arguments about how gun control will solve all our nation's problems.

The most popular among the progressives' arguments is the notion that gun ownership is correlated to gun-related crimes. By their

reasoning, outlawing guns will lead to a drastic reduction in crime. The only problem with this theory, of course, is it never works out the way progressives predict.

While progressives like to come to hearings on gun control with their anti-gun emotions, I prefer to come prepared with the facts. I often rely on a study in Applied Economics Letters, which found, "assault weapons bans did not significantly affect murder rates at the state level," and furthermore revealed, "states with restrictions on the carrying of concealed weapons had higher gun-related murders."[4] Despite all the hysterics we hear from progressives, gun control laws actually increase the rate of gun-related murders. If progressives' true aim was to reduce gun-related murders and crime, they would abandon their gun-control agenda.

Progressives often make the false claim that gun owners purchase a firearm for nefarious purposes, but in fact, it is the opposite. More than two-thirds of gun owners say they own a gun for self-protection. Media commentator John Stossel has provided the clearest explanation of the relationship between crime spikes and gun control laws. "Criminals don't obey the law…. Without the fear of retaliation from victims who might be packing heat, criminals in possession of these [illegal] weapons now have a much easier job…. As the saying goes, 'If guns are outlawed, only outlaws will have guns.'"[5]

Another argument progressives put forth is gun control laws will lower suicide rates. Suicide prevention is a worthy cause. The best way of reducing the number of suicides, however, has nothing to do with restricting gun ownership. Studies show gun control has been ineffective at reducing suicides across the globe. Lithuania is a good example. The country has one of the lowest gun ownership rates—only 0.7 guns per hundred people—but the suicide rate was one of the highest at 34.1 per hundred thousand people in 2009.

Progressives often ignore the racist roots of gun control laws. Gun control advocates often push for their radical agenda in predominantly black populated cities. Think: Chicago, Baltimore, and Washington, D.C. There is a deep-seated mistrust among progressives, with allowing blacks to protect themselves with a firearm.

Condoleezza Rice, while growing up in Birmingham, Alabama, during KKK attacks on civil rights activists, watched her father defend the community with a gun, and police the neighborhood at night. She has described the experience as the defining reason she is pro-Second Amendment. Harriet Tubman, the famous abolitionist, also understood the importance of firearms. She carried a revolver and used it to help slaves escape to freedom.

Throughout the 20th Century, progressives steadily made the argument the Second Amendment protected a collective right—rather than an individual right—for gun ownership, related narrowly to the existence of militias. Law schools and constitutional classes on college campuses stressed that point over and over, until it became the standard line of thinking in academia. This argument was a pillar of the progressives' plan to implement nationwide gun control.

The U.S. Supreme Court, however, halted the progressives' gun control agenda in 2008, with the landmark *Heller* ruling. The background leading to that decision shows the zeal of the anti-gun lobby. The District of Columbia passed an almost total ban on handgun possession, which most experts considered to be the strictest gun control law in the United States at the time. Of course, progressives couldn't just ban handguns and openly admit their ultimate purpose. So in 1975, the D.C. Council made it a crime to carry an unregistered firearm, and simultaneously prohibited the registration of handguns. The few firearms that could be legally owned had to be "unloaded and disassembled or bound by a trigger lock or similar device."[6]

That's where Dick Heller, a D.C. special policeman, entered the picture. Heller served in the U.S. Army as a paratrooper in the 101st Airborne Division. His Capitol Hill house was shot up twice. Once with bullets flying through his living room window, and once through his front door, in the 1970s. Heller received a license to carry a handgun as a special police officer in D.C., after passing background checks and meeting gun proficiency standards. But D.C. law prohibited him from owning a handgun in his home.

The district denied his application to register a handgun he wanted to keep in his house. He filed a lawsuit to prevent the District of Columbia from banning handguns, as well as its requirement that firearms in the home be kept nonfunctional, even when necessary for self-defense.

When Heller's appeal ended up before the Supreme Court, he happened to be guarding the Supreme Court annex.

In June 2008, Justice Antonin Scalia found on behalf of the majority that Heller could possess a handgun in his D.C. home and the law banning handguns was categorically unconstitutional. A majority opinion summary stated, "The Second Amendment protects an individual right to possess a firearm unconnected with service in a militia, and to use that arm for traditionally lawful purposes, such as self-defense within the home."[7]

Two years after *Heller*, in *McDonald v. Chicago*, the Supreme Court held that the Second Amendment right to keep and bear arms protects individuals from laws passed by state and local governments. And in 2016, in *Caetano v. Massachusetts,* the Court reversed a lower court decision that claimed the Second Amendment does not apply to weapons like stun guns.

When the D.C. Council banned handguns in 1975, followed by Chicago and its suburbs in the 1980s, the stated purpose was to build momentum for a national prohibition of handguns. In 1994, pollster Lou Harris confidently predicted handguns would be outlawed nationwide within two or three years.[8] In the past quarter-century, however, the tide has turned. The prediction that requiring permits for handgun possession in the home would reduce handgun ownership has not come to fruition. Instead, we have seen sixteen states in America adopt a form of constitutional carry, which allows Americans to legally carry a concealed gun in public without a permit. Not surprisingly, violent crime has decreased in America as gun ownership has increased.

The *Heller* opinion debunks much of the progressive theory of a collective right by examining English law before the American Revolution and early American laws at about the time the Bill of Rights passed. As tensions increased between the British government and colonists in the mid-eighteenth century, authorities in Massachusetts encouraged citizens to arm themselves. Several newspapers argued this activity was legal because, as British subjects, "the privilege of possessing arms is expressly recognized by the British Bill of Rights,"[9] while another newspaper said this "is a natural right which the people have reserved to themselves, confirmed by the Bill of Rights, to keep arms for their own defense." The second newspaper quoted Sir William Blackstone's influential 18th century Commentaries on the Laws of England, which said "having and using arms for self-preservation and defense" were among the "absolute rights of individuals."[10] Forgotten is the historical context, that centuries ago, in England, parents taught their children how to use longbows; they were readied to enter the militia, to fight invasions. There was always a dearly held responsibility for people to protect themselves, a concept carried over to colonial America, where it was required to arm oneself in the face of Indian ambushes.

During the American debate on the Bill of Rights, and particularly in the discussions about the Second Amendment right to bear arms, many founders were concerned with only allowing arms for a select militia or a politicized army working for a particular political group in America. A citizens' militia was favored by the founders because it would not be controlled by one party or regime. While a select militia served an important national defense purpose, its possible abuse concerned many. Seven of the original thirteen states adopted a bill of rights recognizing the need to arm private citizens for a citizens' militia, or outright recognized an individual right to bear arms. As Richard Henry Lee from Virginia said, "to preserve liberty, it is essential that the whole body of the people always possess arms and be taught alike, especially when young, how to use them."[11]

One of the primary arguments against ratifying the Constitution came from the anti-federalists who opposed a standing army because it empowered the federal government in ways similar to how the kingdoms of Europe stripped rights from the people. The Constitution's advocates, on the other hand, argued that universal armament of the people negated any possible abuse by an army. Noah Webster wrote a pamphlet in favor of ratifying the Constitution, and argued that a standing army is only powerful if the people are disarmed. The federal government wouldn't be able to impose unjust laws, because the people would be armed and would constitute a more powerful force than any group of regular troops.

During the first Congress after ratification of the Constitution, James Madison began work on the Bill of Rights. Madison gathered proposals from various state constitutions and worked on condensing these proposals. His proposed second amendment read, "The right of the people to keep and bear arms shall not be infringed; a well armed and well regulated militia being the best security of a free country; but no person religiously scrupulous of bearing arms shall be compelled to render military service in person."[12] A clause referencing a potential conscientious objector, was removed because of a concern it might be abused by a large group to avoid defending the country.

The House passed the amendment with its current wording, "A well regulated militia, being necessary to the security of a free state, the right of the people to keep and bear arms, shall not be infringed." This language passed the Senate after rejecting a significant amendment that would have only allowed the right to bear arms for the common defense. It is clear from the legislative history and early interpretation the Second Amendment meant to protect an individual's right to bear arms.

As Patrick Henry stated, "The great object is that every man be armed" and "everyone who is able may have a gun."[13] Similarly, William H. Sumner sent a letter to John Adams in 1823, saying that if the population of the United States, "like that of Europe, chiefly consisted of an unarmed peasantry,"[14] it would be conquerable. "Here," he went on, "every house is a castle, and every man a soldier. Arms are in every hand, confidence in every mind, and courage in every heart. It depends upon its own will, and not upon the force of the enemy, whether such a country shall ever be conquered."[15]

It is clear the founders and most Americans alive at the time understood the right to self-defense is a necessary corollary to the God-given right to life, as proclaimed in the Declaration of Independence and protected by the Bill of Rights. Certainly, progressive leaders understand this. As they argue for stripping guns from other Americans, these legislators often have armed police officers protecting them. Even Senator Dianne Feinstein from California, an ardent gun control advocate, carried a concealed handgun when she received death threats and when her home was attacked by the World Liberation Front in the 1970s.

The progressives' approach to the Second Amendment is indicative of their overall attitude toward our individual rights. For them, the only rights that matter are the invented rights belonging to the collective, or community, not the individual rights protected in the Constitution. It should hardly surprise us they reject the individual's right to bear arms, and instead misread a collective, public right to protection in the Second Amendment.

Their repeated assertion that the right to bear arms is limited to members of the militia ignores the context of the Bill of Rights. James Madison's language, "the right to bear arms," is situated in the midst of individual rights within the Bill of Rights, and notably, not within the two clauses in Article I, Section 8, Clauses 15 and 16, which are devoted to the militia. Our founders exercised fastidious attention to detail with these matters. It is not a mere coincidence the right to bear arms, which British Law recognized as an individual and natural right, was placed in the heart of our individual rights in the Bill of Rights.

Conservatives defend the Second Amendment for the same reason progressives want to dismantle it—it is the ultimate individual protection, and it creates a healthy barrier between the individual and an encroaching federal government. The progressives don't trust individuals to make life-saving decisions with guns; they leave it to the government to control who has access to guns.

An armed citizen is a threat to the progressives' agenda. An armed citizen is symbolic of everything we know about individual liberty. While the state and police can play a key role in reinforcing the rule of law, individuals are the first line in self-defense. When I worked as a prosecutor in Colorado, police officers would often repeat a comment that has helped shape my views of guns. Said one officer: "It might take a police officer ten minutes to get to a crime scene, but the victim may only have thirty seconds to respond." Guns can, and do, save lives in those minutes while the police are racing to get to the scene.

At the end of the day, the progressives' assault on guns and their push for gun control isn't about safety or protecting individuals. It is about control. There is a good reason progressives use the terminology "gun control." This effort to eliminate private gun ownership is closely linked to their overall agenda of control and their broader attempt to grow the size and scope of the federal government. Over the years, I've tried to counteract their attempt at control with my own effort in the opposite direction, seeking to restore the Second Amendment right to bear arms for nonviolent felons. This goes back to my days as a DA, when experience taught me a fundamental lesson: the best predictor of future violent behavior is past violent behavior.

As a member of Congress, I've supported bills restoring citizens' rights to bear arms after hearing, early on, the sad tale of an elderly constituent. When he was a college student, he wrote a bad check to his landlord, the result of which was a felony conviction. All these years later, now about sixty years old, he wanted to go hunting with his grandson. But couldn't.

Arizona has sought to do something about similar situations. In 2000, Thomas Yoxall was convicted of felony theft, but after completing probation, his gun rights were restored a few years later. As it turned out, that was a good thing for State Trooper Edward Andersson.

In January of 2017, Yoxall was driving with his wife on his way to California, along a deserted expanse of Interstate 10, in the predawn hours, when he happened upon the state trooper, who had just been shot in the chest and shoulder and was being slammed into the ground by an attacker.

Yoxall recalled retrieving his handgun, saying, "I noticed the suspect on top of Trooper Andersson, beating him in a savage way. I immediately pulled over. My commands were ignored by the suspect as [Andersson] called out for help. And I alleviated the threat to him."[16]

Yoxall fired at the suspect, who charged at the Good Samaritan, who fired again, killing him.

"I firmly believe that that morning I was put there...by God," Yoxall recalled. "It's difficult to think about that day still. I am just thankful that I was able to respond with the courage, dignity, grace, and poise that ultimately saved Trooper Andersson's life."[17]

It's that kind of courage and grace that harkens back to the Texians of yore, who, like Yoxall, stood their ground and pronounced: "Come and take it."

CHAPTER 10

Nullification

"By your gracious cooperation in the transition process, you have shown a watching world that we are a united people pledged to maintaining a political system which guarantees individual liberty to a greater degree than any other."[1]

—RONALD REAGAN

It was a Tuesday on January 20, 1981, when Ronald Reagan placed his hand on the Bible passed down from his mother, taking the oath of office as the fortieth president of the United States.

In his inaugural address, the new president stood beaming at the podium, in a dark suit and silver tie, and began by saying, "To a few of us here today this is a solemn and most momentous occasion. And, yet, in the history of our nation it is a commonplace occurrence. The orderly transfer of authority as called for in the Constitution routinely takes place as it has for almost two centuries and few of us stop to think how unique we really are."[2]

With the practiced voice of a seasoned public speaker, President Reagan punctuated the word *unique*, as if to underscore the remarkable experiment that is America, before finishing the thought: "In the eyes of many in the world," he said, "this every-four-year ceremony we accept as normal is nothing less than a miracle."[3]

Reagan's statement was true enough. And never has the orderly transfer of authority been so tested as it is being tested as I write this in 2020.

Even before President Trump took office, when his ascension to the Oval Office was confirmed by the electorate, the progressives launched a withering assault on his presidency, seeking to dig up dirt, attempting to delegitimize his election, foiling his administration at every turn, employing the entrenched Washington bureaucracy to undermine his policies, and enlisting the left-leaning media in what can only be described as a nullification of the executive branch and circumvention of our constitutional right to elect our national leader.

As in other eras, what the progressives are grasping for now is nothing less than unauthorized control, wresting it away from We the People.

James Madison, the founding father and driving force behind our Constitution, foresaw the potential for an unaccountable government, which is why, drawing on Montesquieu's theories, he built in the separation of powers among the branches of government.

"The accumulation of all powers, legislative, executive and judiciary in the same hands, whether of one, or few, or many, and whether hereditary, self-appointed or elective, may justly be pronounced the very definition of tyranny," Madison wrote.[4]

What we are witnessing now, some two centuries later, is the rising force of that tyranny from the left.

* * *

From the beginning, what distinguished Trump from any previous president—he is the ultimate outsider, with no political curriculum vitae, apart from even other veteran Republicans. Trump was, at an essential level, a disruptor. He campaigned on one central issue: draining the swamp, which was campaign speak for dismantling the administrative state—a shadow government—built by progressives such as Wilson, FDR, and those who succeeded them. The progressives have worked for a century to create an entrenched bureaucracy—what some call the "deep state"—as a way to create permanent progressivism, regardless which party is in control of Congress or the White House. Trump, to say the least, was not an establishment candidate. Mitt Romney was. George W. Bush was. There is a difference between being a Republican and being a disruptor who refuses to abide by the Washington norms of establishment politics.

Trump represented such a threat that, during his campaign, Obama political appointees were already on the attack, seeking federal court orders to spy on Trump associates, and then leaking those names to the media.

Meanwhile, as we now know, Trump's chief rival for the presidency, Hillary Clinton, sought to obtain dirt on Trump, true or concocted. A Clinton campaign attorney hired an opposition research firm, which in turn, hired a former British MI6 spy to create a damaging dossier from supposed Russian government sources. The Democrats tried to hide their involvements while false stories were spoon-fed to willing members of the FBI.

Attacks on Trump resumed in the immediate aftermath of his victory at the ballot box when a phalanx of Clinton supporters urged her to challenge the results, particularly in three key battleground states—Wisconsin, Michigan, and Pennsylvania—that turned the tide in Trump's favor.

The progressives suggested there was evidence the election was rigged. Jill Stein, the Green Party candidate, called for a recount. "After a divisive and painful presidential race, reported hacks into voter and party databases and individual email accounts are causing many Americans to wonder if our election results are reliable," Stein said. "These concerns need to be investigated before the 2016 presidential election is certified. We deserve elections we can trust."[5]

For her effort, Stein raised more than $2.5 million in a single day to pay for those election challenges.

Other challenges to Trump's presidency continued unabated when Democrats boycotted his inauguration. "I do not plan to attend the inauguration," said Rep. John Lewis, a Georgia Democrat who held a seat since 1987. "It will be the first one that I miss since I've been in the Congress."[6]

What Lewis was declaring was a historic break from tradition; after the battle of a presidential campaign, both sides have typically laid down their proverbial swords to take their places at the Capitol to witness the swearing in of our nation's elected leader, before retiring to a bipartisan luncheon for the newly installed president and vice president.

Dozens of other Democrats followed suit, however, refusing to attend the ceremony as a symbol of their protest. It was nothing short of an attempt to undermine Trump's presidency before it began. And it was, from my view, wrong. I was never a fan of Barack Obama or his progressive policies, but I didn't boycott his State of the Union addresses in 2015 and 2016. Had I been elected to Congress when Obama was inaugurated in 2009 and 2013, I would've been there. There's a simple reason: We show respect for the office, not the person.

That isn't the way of the progressives. Rebellion from the left was swiftly followed by widespread calls for violence against Trump, the new president. Celebrities were especially emboldened in their extremism, advocating for harming or killing Trump, not to mention whipping up support for a military coup or bombing the White House.

Among the more notable suggestions, comedian Kathy Griffin held up a bloodied mask in the likeness of Trump beheaded. Rapper Snoop Dogg pointed a gun at a clown dressed as Trump. Actor Mickey Rourke wielded a baseball bat as a way to beat the president. At the Women's March in Washington, D.C., pop singer Madonna said, "Yes, I'm angry. Yes, I'm outraged. Yes, I have thought an awful lot about blowing up the White House, but I know that this won't change anything."[7]

Academy-award winning actor Robert De Niro weighed in as well, feeling no compunctions about saying of Trump: "He's a punk, he's a dog, he's a pig, he's a con, he's a bull----t artist, a mutt who doesn't know what he's talking about, doesn't do his homework, doesn't care, thinks he's gaming society, doesn't pay his taxes. He's an embarrassment to this country. He talks [about] how he wants to punch people in the face.... I'd like to punch him in the face."[8]

On the Late Show, host Stephen Colbert took aim at the president, displaying the severed head of White House senior adviser Stephen Miller on a pike. Comedian Sarah Silverman put a cap on things with her suggestion of a military coup to oust Trump from the White House.

There was nothing funny about that. Such vitriol was unthinkable during past administrations, even only four years earlier, when decorum for the office prevailed. Imagine what would have happened had people pilloried Obama when he became the new president, the same way Trump experienced it. It's a sad state of affairs that progressives, though, find humor in talking about bringing harm to our president now. And the irony isn't lost on me that the people who call my office, asking why I'm not more bipartisan, are the same people who laughed at Kathy Griffin holding up a beheaded president.

* * *

In the first blush of his presidency, Trump faced not just widespread ridicule, but deep state resistance from those within the beltway, working for the federal government but refusing, in large and small ways, to accept the transition of power.

In a symbolic gesture presaging trouble to follow, some federal workers refused to hang the portrait of Trump in the public spaces of their offices, as is customary in federal buildings. Perhaps it shouldn't have been a surprise, given that nearly all political contributions from federal workers were directed to Clinton's failed campaign.

Early on, Trump was compelled to fire Sally Yates, his acting attorney general, for insubordination. She instructed Justice Department officials not to defend Trump's executive order, a temporary ban on the admission of refugees and a travel ban from some other countries. Yates "betrayed the Department of Justice by refusing to enforce a legal order designed to protect the citizens of the United States," the White House stated.[9]

A growing number of career bureaucrats in the Interior Department and Environmental Protection Agency, as well as staffers within the intelligence agencies, defied the Oval Office, essentially asserting themselves as a fourth branch of government, a permanent, unelected but invisible resistance, which had the effect of foiling the agenda of a president elected by the people. Even the liberal *New York Times*, in an October 2019 article, couldn't deny the existence of a "deep state" in quiet conflict with and generating great hostility toward President Trump.

The startling headline: "Trump's War on the 'Deep State' Turns Against Him." The article provided further explanation, saying, "The impeachment inquiry is in some ways the culmination of a battle between the president and the government institutions he distrusted and disparaged."[10]

What the *Times* reported was a remarkable acknowledgement that a sitting president was the subject of insurrection from within the executive branch of government he heads. The article went on to say, "The House impeachment inquiry into Mr. Trump's efforts to force Ukraine to investigate Democrats is the climax of a thirty-three-month scorched-earth struggle between a president with no record of public service and the government he inherited but never trusted."[11]

Even in that statement, the *New York Times* couldn't hide its own bias, jabbing that Trump had "no record of public service," as if such a gap in his resume was justification for the insurrection against him and the will of the people who elected him president.

Resistance within the administrative state wasn't a surprise, not only because of Trump's role as a disruptor, but also because many government workers were holdovers from the Obama administration or longstanding political creatures of the progressive state, threatened by Trump's call to drain the swamp that is Washington.

As a congressman, I've become all too familiar with the way members of one party or another will seek to preserve their power by stashing like-minded government workers into policy-making positions whenever a new administration takes over in Washington. That's why I introduced, along with Democrat Ted Lieu of California, a bipartisan measure called the Political Appointee Burrowing Prevention Act.

The idea was to make sure a political appointee couldn't simply slide into a career civil service position for at least two years—a cooling-off period. "Our federal civil service's hiring process is supposed to be a competitive, merit-based system where the best and brightest are considered based on their ability to do the job, not their political affiliation," I said, when the bill advanced though the House in March 2018. "Political appointees are supposed to serve the president's agenda for a temporary period of time, and part of their duty is to know when to step down from their position of power. This bill ensures that agencies hire career civil servants that are the most qualified, not the most politically connected."[12]

That career bureaucrats—elected to nothing, voted in by no one— would seek to circumvent our constitutional process, to impose their own policies over the president's was a grave concern dating back to our founding fathers, Madison in particular. The chief author of the Constitution, Madison, recognized the threat to past societies—the great empires of Rome and Athens—which he said, "succumbed to demagoguery from misfits, and crumbled from mob rule."

Anticipating our modern political dilemma, Madison referenced the threat of "renegade" politicians who advocated for violence. "When a band of debtors can force the abolition of debt, and equal division of property, a mob can destroy the government by populist rage," he said.

The "misfits" that concerned Madison two centuries ago emerged early in Trump's presidency, including James Comey, the ex-FBI director, who testified in a Senate hearing that he leaked a memo he wrote about a conversation he had held with the president.

"My judgment was, I needed to get that out into the public square, and so I asked a friend of mine to share the content of the memo with a reporter," Comey told the Senate Intelligence Committee. "[I] didn't do it myself for a variety of reasons, but I asked him to, because I thought that might prompt the appointment of the special counsel."[13]

Comey's admission is stunning on its face. And yet leaks emerged from all sides after Trump took office—to the applause of many in the establishment, exhorted by the media, even when the exposed information was sensitive, classified, or of national security. To wit: *The Columbia Journalism Review* declared, "Flynn resignation shows leaks under Trump are working. Keep 'em coming."

If I ever thought the EPA had the most entrenched liberal bureaucrats in a federal agency, the events of the recent past have demonstrated it is actually the intelligence and foreign policy bureaucracies where not only the leaks have sprung, but where the progressive agenda burrowed in to resist Trump.

* * *

The withering assault on Trump, of course, came with calls for his impeachment from the day he took office on January 20, 2017. "The campaign to impeach Donald Trump has already begun," a *Washington Post* headline blared, on that day.[14]

"The impeachment drive comes as Democrats and liberal activists are mounting broad opposition to stymie Trump's agenda," the *Post* journalist wrote.[15]

Within four months, several members of Congress called for Trump's impeachment. "Republicans should step up to the plate and confront the fact that this president appears to be unstable," said Representative Maxine Waters.[16]

Calls for Trump's removal continued into the summer of 2017, when Democratic Congressman Steve Cohen from Tennessee said he would introduce articles of impeachment because the president "failed the presidential test of moral leadership."[17]

Cohen and several other Democrats introduced five articles of impeachment on November 15, with Cohen saying, Trump's "train of injuries must be brought to an end." Cohen's accusations ranged from violating the emoluments clause to "undermining the independence of the federal judiciary" to "undermining the freedom of the press."[18]

Eventually, the move to impeach stuck after an anonymous whistleblower—a creature of the deep state—filed a complaint, alleging that Trump pressured Ukraine to investigate his political rival, Democrat Joe Biden, the former vice president, and his son Hunter. Trump was accused of withholding military aid to Ukraine in what was alleged to be a quid pro quo campaign of seeking a favor in exchange for a favor. Democrat Nancy Pelosi, the House Speaker, launched the impeachment inquiry on September 24, 2019.

Whatever history may ultimately prove, this much is already self-evident about the progressives' full-throttle push to impeach the president: they engaged in a biased process to achieve a biased result.

Nothing about the process could have yielded the truth; it was designed to create a political outcome, the removal of the president.

The move to oust Trump was accompanied by unprecedented negative news about him. This isn't opinion; nonpartisan media research firms concluded 90 percent of all news about the president cast him in a negative light. Out the window went objective reporting. Reporters covering the White House could barely contain their contempt in what were supposed to be news columns, not opinion pieces.

Wikileaks proved as much, demonstrating how some writers from those news organizations colluded with the progressives, while fake news proliferated, spreading outrageous lies about, among other things, Trump planning to invade Mexico, or how he removed a bust of Martin Luther King Jr. from the West Wing.

The extremity of the wild news stories reached the height of absurdity when the *Huffington Post* ran—and then retracted—a piece calling for Trump's execution, in June 2017. "Trump must be prosecuted—if convicted in a court of law—executed," the story declared, before it was taken down from the site.[19]

The fever pitch to assail Trump got to the point that a Yale psychiatrist, without even meeting or diagnosing the president in person, was trotted out before Congress to make the outrageous claim Trump was psychologically unfit to continue as chief executive. Adding insanity to the assessment, the psychiatrist opined on whether the president could be restrained as part of an examination. Was this a therapist, or an arm breaker from the former Soviet Union, seeking to extract a confession?

The specter of the Twenty-Fifth Amendment—replacing the president with the vice president—arose in August 2017, when Rep. Jackie Speier, a California Democrat, called for Trump's removal. The amendment allows the vice president and two-thirds of the president's cabinet to declare the president unfit. Speier—who was left for dead after being shot five times in the Jonestown massacre of 1978—said, what Trump has shown is "erratic behavior and lack of mental capacity."[20]

Vanity Fair appeared to take a cue from Speier's broadside, publishing a shrill piece that October by Gabe Sherman, headlined with the sensational: "'I hate everyone in the White House!' Trump Seethes As Advisers Fear the President is 'Unraveling.'"[21]

Sherman's anonymously sourced piece offered this outrageous depiction:

> [S]ome West Wing advisers were worried that Trump's behavior could cause the Cabinet to take extraordinary Constitutional measures to remove him from office. Several months ago, according to two sources with knowledge of the conversation, former chief strategist Steve Bannon told Trump that the risk to his presidency wasn't impeachment, but the 25th Amendment—the provision by which a majority of the Cabinet can vote to remove the president. When Bannon mentioned the 25th Amendment, Trump said, 'What's that?' According to a source, Bannon has told people he thinks Trump has only a 30 percent chance of making it the full term.[22]

The all-out war against Trump extended to his allies. That included Ajit Pai, chairman of the FCC, a bureaucratic agency built in the image of the progressives who created it. The agency controlled the airwaves and internet with little accountability to the public. Pai sought to undo the cumbersome regulations of what are known as net neutrality, bringing a constitutional perspective to what the agency exists to do. The response to this Trump ally was in line with the mob-like response to Trump.

Pai, who supports conservative principles, was called a pedophile and a "dirty, sneaky Indian" who should go back to where he came from. Anonymous rants online threatened to kill Pai and his family. Protestors stalked Pai's driveway, which prompted him to say, they "come up to our front windows and take photographs of the inside of the house. My kids are five and three. It's not pleasant."[23]

That Pai and his positions on telecommunications policy could inspire such vicious responses only speaks to the draconian tactics of the left, which are ratcheted up even further when it comes to attacking President Trump.

Vicious rants against Trump political supporters, not surprisingly, extended to many others in the president's orbit, including Sarah Sanders, then the White House press secretary, who was summarily kicked out of a restaurant, along with her family, by the left-wing owner. Early one morning, protestors besieged Kirstjen Nielsen, then secretary of the Department of Homeland Security, at her Alexandria, Virginia townhouse. Posters with her image darkened read: "RESIGN." [24]A Chicago bar went so far as to refuse to serve Trump backers.

In June of 2018, Representative Maxine Waters, the California Democrat who called Trump "unstable," urged people to "turn on" Trump officials, to "harass" them, and ensure they "they won't be able to go to a restaurant, they won't be able to stop at a gas station, they're not going to be able to shop at a department store."[25]

Even Trump donors became fair game in the vicious call-out culture espoused by the left. In August 2019, Representative Joaquin Castro, a Texas Democrat, tweeted out a list of Trump donors to shame them publicly.

"Sad to see," Castro tweeted about the group of Trump contributors.[26]

Representative Dan Crenshaw, a Texas Republican, denounced Castro, calling his actions a form of "fascism."[27] Castro responded by saying he was merely putting out what was already public information about donors. But tell that to a woman who donated to Trump and found herself on the receiving end of a voicemail denouncing her as a racist and making threats against her.

* * *

This is what we've come to, where resistance has devolved into nullification of Trump—the extent of which we haven't witnessed since the eve of the Civil War. It was back in the lead up to the war between the states when the great orator, John C. Calhoun, the senator from South Carolina, became the architect of a policy called "nullification." It stipulated that federal law not in the best interests of a state could be dismissed by that state without punishment. Calhoun sought to prevent the union from fracturing into civil war, but he also strenuously argued that a state had the right to secede from the union to retain its liberty.

Nullification, of course, has taken on a different dimension in today's rough-hewn political brawls where, for progressives, anything goes. The fight over illegal immigration is telling. Whenever federal authorities sought to detain an illegal alien, as required by law, the media became inflamed. Progressives castigated Trump, even though what his administration was doing was simply upholding the law of the land. It shouldn't go without notice that some of those who were deported also happened to have been convicted of voter fraud, identity theft, or other crimes. Suddenly, though, progressives spoke moralistically about how the illegal alien was somehow victimized, without regard to fundamental laws, about the integrity of our borders and protecting them.

Why is it a cause celeb for the progressives to tout the rights of those who are living in the United States illegally, without paying taxes, while in fact, some do harbor prior criminal records? Why is it suddenly outrageous to enforce our laws, to protect our borders? Liberals cloak their outrage in the language of righteousness, in an extreme form of political correctness, but it is hollow. Liberals latched onto the conception of nullification to fight against efforts to uphold federal immigrant laws. They clothed their repudiation of U.S. law with the benign sounding "sanctuary city." That included New Haven, for instance, which handed out government I.D. cards to illegal aliens, never mind it was a violation of federal law.

"Sanctuary city" laws were adopted by nearly five hundred American cities, repudiating federal immigration law. In late 2019, the U.S. Justice Department filed a petition asking the Supreme Court to hear arguments in a case against California, which was openly defying federal immigration law.

This is how far we've fallen, with cities and states openly defying the rule of law, celebrities calling for the execution of the president, a deep state of entrenched government bureaucrats working to undermine the executive branch, and members of Congress seeking to invalidate a national election the moment it produces a result they don't like.

Progressives, lest it be forgotten, see the bureaucratic machinery in Washington as a way of protecting America from policies of a president they hate. Lest it be forgotten, the progressives created a shadow government comprised of government careerists decades earlier as a way of circumventing Congress—and our Constitution. This, by the way, explains why the progressives leveled such a vicious attack when federal judge Brett Kavanaugh was nominated to the high court; Kavanaugh has demonstrated throughout his tenure as a judge, a laser-like focus on scaling back the administrative state.

James Madison, for one, was keenly on guard against threats to our republican form of government. While he never identified the deep state as one such threat, he was, nevertheless, aware of how the "mob" and "misfits" in a pure democracy could undermine our Constitution.

Though he was the chief architect of our Constitution, he remains an elusive figure in the Capitol; we find his figure not there, but at the Library of Congress, perched on a thirty-ton mass of marble imported from Italy. Even a plaster model of his sculpture, located within the U.S. Capitol building, is not on public view. Never more than now do we need reminders of his caution against tyranny.

Madison's presence, however, can be found if we look hard enough. There he is, in a Capitol painting of the signing of our Constitution, hanging in the East Grand Stairway. Madison is seated to the right of Benjamin Franklin, which is all too appropriate. For it was Franklin who, on July 20, 1787, addressed the Constitutional Conventional with his thoughts about whether the Constitution should permit the impeachment of the president.

A prolific note-taker, Madison's transcription from the convention reflects: "Docr. Franklin was for retaining the clause as favorable to the executive." He noted Franklin's comment: "'History furnishes one example only of a Magistrate being formally brought to public Justice.' Every body cried out [against] this as unconstitutional." Madison's notes show the continuation of Franklin's thoughts on this topic: "'What was the practice before this in cases where the chief Magistrate rendered himself obnoxious? Why recourse was had to assassination in which he was not only deprived of his life, but of the opportunity of vindicating his character. It would be the best way therefore to provide the Constitution for the regular punishment of the Executive when his misconduct should deserve it, and for his honorable acquittal when he should be unjustly accused."[28]

The founders carefully considered impeachment and the methods for holding the executive accountable. Modern-day progressives, however, have subverted the accountability structure, and in so doing, have undermined the fundamentals of our political process. The task for us today is to set aside divisive politics and recommit ourselves to the principles that make the United States exceptional.

CHAPTER 11

It Wasn't Always This Way

"To render us again one people, acting as one nation, should be the object of every man really a patriot."[1]

—THOMAS JEFFERSON

As a child joins my Capitol tour, I'll whisper to the youngster, "When I ask you a question, just say, *thirteen*."

So I begin: "How many original colonies, young lady?"

On cue, she answers: "Thirteen."

"How many statues in the crypt?"

"Thirteen"

"Right again."

When we arrive at the U.S. flag draped just off the rotunda, I say, "How many red and white stripes on the flag?"

There's that magic number again: thirteen.

I use the flag during the visitors' discussion, as a transition to examine the most consequential subject on the tour—unity. We have thirteen stripes on the flag and fifty stars, one for each of the states in our union. I ask my guests about the underlying symbolism. We, as Americans, believe our flag represents our unity. Our flag is a symbol of our history, and a reminder of how our thirteen original colonies, each with distinct characteristics, joined to form the United States. The flag also symbolizes how we are united in purpose in this experiment in self-government.

As further evidence of our unity, I mention the preamble to our Constitution: *We the people of the United States, in order to form a more perfect union...*

First, I point out we are the United States, not a federation, like Europe, or a cartel, like OPEC.

Second, I emphasize our people must be united in spirit, values, and duty, just as the states are united by geography, federal laws, and necessity.

As we stand in the rotunda, I direct my guests' attention upward to the apotheosis of George Washington. Encircling Washington's spirit ascending to heaven are, yes, thirteen female figures in flowing robes. A few of the women are clutching a banner. I usually pause at this point so the guests can strain to read what is written on the banner. Then, when they can't, I tell them: *E Pluribus Unum*. Latin for "out of many, one."

"How many letters in that Latin phrase?" I ask my young assistant. "Thirteen"—what else?

I stress to my guests the Latin phrase is one of the most echoed in the Capitol building. It appears on the ceiling in the House chambers. It is emblazoned on a panel behind the vice president's chair in the Senate chambers. *E Pluribus Unum* is engraved on the cast iron pedestal of the freedom statute atop the dome.

E Pluribus Unum portrays more than a union of states with proximate geographical boundaries. The simple expression provides clues about our national DNA. Our states have different topography, economic priorities, and history. Our people are from different racial groups and ancestral ties, and we hold vastly different political views. But our diverse people have always come together in support of personal freedom and individual property rights. We are a collection of various and distinct backgrounds that unite to form a powerful national identity.

We see the same sun rise every morning, that George Washington and his troops witnessed at Valley Forge. We breathe the same air as the slaves when they were freed after the Emancipation Proclamation. We felt the same surge of anger and patriotism in the wake of the September 11, 2001, terrorist attacks our parents and grandparents felt after the attack on Pearl Harbor. *E Pluribus Unum* has come to mean one people from many backgrounds, united to defend the experiment our founders created, and to continue defending our individual liberty.

The motto also represents how we are connected to our forefathers and to the generations of Americans who lived before and who helped make America what it is today. *E Pluribus Unum* extends across racial lines, socio-economic, and geographic boundaries—and even across time. We are, in that regard, unified with our nation's founding generation.

E Pluribus Unum also reminds us of the famous words often attributed to Benjamin Franklin, who is believed to have uttered, in the Continental Congress: "We must, indeed, all hang together, or most assuredly, we shall all hang separately." He was referencing the risk of being executed for treason, which our founders assumed in joining the rebellion against the British crown. Unity was more than a lofty ideal; it was necessary for their individual survival, and for the survival of the new nation.

Our founders' focus on unity contrasts with the divisive identity politics we see today. Our strong political identity as a freedom-loving people has helped us overcome our vast differences in ethnicity and national origins. Many Americans today can trace their roots to other nationalities by only going back a few generations. The result is one of the most beautiful aspects of American citizenship. One can *become* an American in ways not possible elsewhere. Becoming an American is to take part in a political experiment and to join three centuries of individuals coalescing to resist the threat of tyranny. Our immigration system reflects this difference, and we see immigrants to our country able to assimilate faster than those of other countries.

If you don't believe me, just look at the struggles of Middle Eastern and African immigrants in Europe. For generations to come, these immigrants to Europe, and their children and grandchildren, will feel different and set apart, not fully integrated into their new home country. This, of course, isn't owing to their own actions, but to those of countries that are not accustomed, as America is, to welcoming newcomers, as symbolized by the Statue of Liberty. From our shores, we have embraced generations from the famines of Ireland, from war-torn Vietnam, and elsewhere.

I understand this dynamic at an intimate level; my grandparents on my mother's side immigrated to the United States from Norway, and the first thing they wanted to do as Americans was to lose their accents. They pronounced "James" as "Yames." It wasn't that they were ashamed of their Norwegian heritage; one of my relatives was a Norwegian resistance fighter who was caught by the Nazis and thrown in a concentration camp before he was freed a few months later. There was great pride in my grandparents when they became Americans and worked two jobs to raise my mother. They always flew the American flag at their home.

They never lost their accent. But they were Americans, plain and simple.

Before their time, President Woodrow Wilson, a progressive through and through, who sought to bend the Constitution to his designs, oversaw unprecedented segregation in federal offices. But he also needed to rally the melting pot of American immigrants, if only for expedience's sake, so they would fight united under the American flag; Wilson understood the importance of assimilation when he said, "You cannot become thorough

Americans if you think of yourselves in groups. America does not consist of groups. A man who thinks of himself as belonging to a particular national group has not yet become an American."[2]

Wilson's invocation is a far cry from today's inflammatory identity politics preached on college campuses, infused with the rhetoric of division, cloaked in a specious righteousness.

Lost in today's hate-filled echo chamber is Katherine Lee Bates's 1895 poem, "Pikes Peak," which became the lyrics for the song "America the Beautiful." In just one line, Bates summarized the American ethos. That famous line is printed in the Cox corridor: "America! God shed His grace on thee, and crown thy good with brotherhood from sea to shining sea!" Americans have aspired to brotherhood from Maine to California, Washington to Florida, recognizing that God blessed this great land with abundance.

There are plenty of documented instances where particular Americans did not live up to this idea, particularly in their treatment of African slaves, Native Americans, Mormons, and Roman Catholics. But our highest aspirations united us to recognize the wisdom in Psalm 133:1, "How good and pleasant it is when God's people live together in unity."

Until the past few decades, American liberals used the language of inclusion. The loudest voices and intellectual leaders on the left called for Americans to come together and provide equal opportunity for all. In his "I have a dream speech," in 1963, the Reverend Martin Luther King, Jr. reaffirmed the principles of our founding documents: "When the architects of our republic wrote the magnificent words of the Constitution and the Declaration of Independence, they were signing a promissory note to which every American was to fall heir. This note was a promise that all men—yes, black men as well as white men—would be guaranteed the unalienable rights of life, liberty, and the pursuit of happiness."[3]

King believed the devastation of slavery could be healed through unity, through blacks and whites working together. In contrast to the divisive and ugly identity politics we see today, King's identity politics rested on our identity as Americans, with a common goal.

Over the course of our nation's existence, many insightful foreigners have recognized unity as America's strength. An example can be seen in a famous 1851 painting depicting George Washington crossing the Delaware River for a surprise attack on Hessian troops, the day after Christmas, in 1776. Emanuel Leutze completed the twenty-two-foot-wide painting titled *Washington Crossing the Delaware*, in 1851.

As a German immigrant to America, Leutze fell in love with American history and culture, and his painting reflected his views of the prevailing sentiment in our country. In addition to Washington, the occupants of the rowboat included a frontiersman, a Scot, a black man, a woman disguised as a man, two farmers, a native American, a politician—founding father James Monroe—and an immigrant soldier, General Edward Hand. Leutze's painting depicts a diverse group of countrymen—and woman—with a variety of American backgrounds and stories, uniting to fight for freedom.

It wasn't so long ago when I saw a replica of this painting for the first time, in Republican Leader Kevin McCarthy's office in the Capitol building as he pointed out the different figures to me. In a twist of fate, the original painting remained in a German art gallery for years, and was destroyed in a British bombing raid during World War II. The joke is, England finally got its revenge for the Revolutionary war.

Us vs. Them

The American sense of unity, and our thirteen-letter Latin slogan, are under attack in America, on a scale not seen since the Civil War.

The conflict used to be North versus South, slave owner against abolitionist. Now the battle is being waged by modern-day progressives and their Marxist cousins, against conservatives. The left is following the playbook written by their radical predecessors who sought to sow the seeds of division in America.

To fully grasp the tensions existing in America today, it is necessary to go at least as far back as World War II. Following the war, an uneasy alliance prevailed among the victorious powers in Europe, Russia, and the United States. Communism and socialism were spreading like a virus around the world, in part, because of a power vacuum caused by military conflict fatigue and diminishing financial resources, the result of poor U.S. economic policy, and expensive ventures around the world. Even with their spreading influence, communists were frustrated that their efforts to reach mainstream Americans were often thwarted by what they regarded as a lack of class consciousness among Americans.

Marxist revolutions necessitate strife among the classes. For Marx, that strife is borne from class consciousness on the part of the proletariat, the working class. That consciousness includes an awareness of one's own exploitation at the hands of the other class, the bourgeoisie, or the capital owners. While class consciousness did not exist in America the way it did in Europe and elsewhere in the world, what did exist, and what leftist activists seized as an opportunity to foment revolution, were the rising social tensions surrounding race issues, women's equality, and growing frustration about the Vietnam War.

The 1960s began with the election of a young, idealistic president, John F. Kennedy. For the first time in decades, America's leader promised to heal a nation tired of war, civil unrest, and economic injustice. President Kennedy's assassination in 1963 led to even greater frustration among those who sought a path forward. Daily, Americans protested and watched protests against the war in Vietnam, unfair treatment of black citizens, and women's inequality. The frustration grew into mass riots as the Reverend Martin Luther King Jr. and Robert Kennedy were murdered.

A discussion of modern social upheaval would be incomplete without mentioning Saul Alinsky, the architect of today's progressive tactics. Alinsky produced a plan for radically transforming America under the benign slogan of social change. His central thesis focused on training organizers to agitate to the point of conflict. Alinsky also taught that there had to be a face associated with the people's discontent; more than just a corporation, it should be a CEO. Not city hall, but a mayor. And ultimately, not a government policy, but a president. Alinsky described the strategy as, "Pick the target, freeze it, personalize it, and polarize it."[4]

To polarize an opponent, Alinsky taught his followers to act as defenders of human decency and to react with moral outrage when the target misspoke. For Alinsky and his followers, it was also important to dismiss your opponent as morally or intellectually deficient.

In his most recognized work, *Rules for Radicals*, Alinsky acknowledged, "the first radical known to man who rebelled against the establishment and did it so effectively that he at least won his own kingdom—Lucifer."[5] This book, with its shocking nod to Satan's rebellion, is the same book President Obama used as a text in some of the classes he instructed, and about which Hillary Clinton wrote her senior thesis in college. She interviewed Alinsky for her project.

If there was any doubt about Alinsky's admiration for Lucifer, he clarified his position during a 1972 interview with *Playboy* magazine, just before his death, saying, "Let's say that if there is an afterlife, and I have anything to say about it, I will unreservedly choose to go to hell….Hell would be heaven for me."[6]

Obama was influenced by Alinsky's work. It wasn't just that Obama's adopted hometown was Alinsky's Chicago, or that Obama surrounded himself with many progressive intellectuals influenced by Alinsky. Obama used divisive identity politics to his advantage and left so many frustrated that he didn't do more to unify America. Obama held little regard for the unified identity of America. In fact, his highest value was on so-called change. He spoke of change in a vague and baffling way. Change was part of his campaign slogan, and it was an oft-recited but never explained chant. As a candidate for president in 2008, Obama promised, "We are five days away from fundamentally transforming the United States of America."[7] His desire to fundamentally transform the greatest country in the world underscored not only his hubris, but his ignorance of the spirit of unity that has made us a great nation.

Just over a decade removed from Obama's inauguration as president, we live in a country more divided, more distracted, and more disjointed than before his intentional design to fundamentally transform America.

The radical progressives have moved away from the inclusive language of the left from previous generations, and they have instead adopted new phrases in line with Alinsky's polarization strategy. Why? Because the progressives are losing. And the more they lose America, the more they seek to employ ever more radical tactics of separation. When a school cafeteria offers burritos for lunch, the progressives deride it as "cultural appropriation." When a Democratic presidential candidate states, "all lives matter," he is pushed off the stage by radicals chanting "black lives matter." A political leader working for Hillary Clinton's campaign suggested Senator Bernie Sanders may be a white supremacist, because Sanders indicated on the campaign trail that voting for a candidate solely because she is a woman of color may be an insufficient reason.

The best examples of shallow political thought censuring free speech can be found where you would least expect to find them—or maybe not. America's college campuses are rife with terms such as "microaggression" and "safe space." The progressives have targeted America's youth with spectacular results. Yale students objected to reading Shakespeare because he was a white male. An Iowa University professor criticized some statues as supporting white supremacy because they were made of white marble. College students in Michigan were jailed for distributing pocket Constitutions. In 2017, a school board in Oregon removed the name *Lynch* from three elementary school buildings because some students and families complained the name made them think of the racist practice of hanging blacks. The school buildings were not named for that practice, though. They were named after a family whose last name was Lynch; over a century ago, the family donated the land for the schools.[8] That same year, ESPN, the giant sports network, pulled an announcer from calling a University of Virginia football game because his name was Robert Lee, apparently for fear of offending people who were upset his name was similar to Confederate General Robert E. Lee. The sportscaster is Asian American. And so it goes.

The word "Nazi" is particularly in vogue lately. Apparently, anyone who disagrees with the progressives is a Nazi. Singer Cher accused the Department of Immigration and Customs Enforcement of using Gestapo tactics.[9] Actor Adam Scott compared Fox News host Tucker Carlson to a Joseph Goebbels, the Nazi leader in Hitler's administration, tasked with overseeing propaganda creation.[10] Donny Deutsch, a regular television commentator, called President Donald Trump a Nazi.[11]

Deutsch certainly isn't alone. Consistent with Alinsky's rule to polarize your opponent, many progressive celebrities have called not just Trump a Nazi, but his supporters as well. The term "Nazi," thanks to progressives, has come to mean anyone who disagrees with progressives. The fact is, radical progressives today engage in bullying and silencing behaviors much more similar to Nazi tactics than do those whom they condemn, but they scream that it is the conservatives who are the Nazis. Alinsky and his followers never let the facts get in the way of a divisive narrative.

The careless "Nazi" label ignores important facts about the president. Are most Israeli Jews Nazi sympathizers since they overwhelmingly support the president? Or are one-third of the voting Jews in America Nazis? How can you call Trump a Nazi when he paid for his daughter's Jewish wedding and blessed her conversion to Judaism, and then welcomed his Jewish daughter and Jewish son-in-law into the White House to work with him as close advisors?

What is unfolding today isn't just about name calling. Progressive attacks are a honed political message of personal destruction. No longer are progressives willing to engage in a reasoned debate in the market-place of ideas that so influenced our founding fathers. With the heated rhetoric of the left, so many are no longer willing to debate, to chal-lenge—to even be wrong and be allowed to adjust their remarks, to fix their mistakes, to make amends. Instead, the progressives rant in height-ened language of condemnation, and the mass media, largely comprised of liberals, eat it up.

If you don't hold the right views—at least, the views foisted on us by progressives—you're not allowed to talk. It's no longer a question of whether your argument is better than your adversary; you're no longer permitted to have the argument. You're shouted down on college campuses. It's all part of the damaging legacy of the Alinsky strategy to polarize. We should condemn those intolerant tactics. Instead, we forget the fundamental idea expressed by our founders—the idea that we are free to speak, to express ourselves, even if others don't agree with it, even if it's offensive to us. That's why, in 1977, the Supreme Court allowed neo-Nazis to march through a largely Jewish area of Illinois.[12] It doesn't matter how offensive it is—whatever it is; it's still speech—and it's free.

Now, though, the mere existence of a Confederate statue inspires some to tear it down—along with the fact of our history. Now you get creamed on Facebook and social media if you don't kowtow to the progressive's program—a phenomenon with which I am all too familiar as a public figure. You're called a sexist because you're pro-life. You're called a racist because you want to secure the border. In the 1990s, Colorado held an anti-gay ballot initiative, and just because Mo Siegel, the founder of Celestial Seasonings, declined to donate to the gay cause, he found his business boycotted.[13] Even nowadays, in major cities across the country, if local businesses decline to participate in the gay pride parade, they are harassed; some businesses are even attacked with death threats. The reign of terror of the progressives extends far and wide.

What we are seeing is a progressive attempt to marginalize conservative thought, when our founding fathers designed ours to be a tolerant society. But the intolerance perpetuated by the left is nothing less than a form of censorship, of thought control, where thuggery and the specter of the mob inspires fear and silence.

Which brings us back to that fundamental concept of our nation—that we are a republic, not a democracy where the mob rules. And yet this is where our nation is heading if we don't put a stop to it. We're going to lose everything that made our nation the premiere land of individual freedom. Good people aren't standing up. And this is wrong.

One of my congressional colleagues made headlines soon after she was sworn in as a freshman member of Congress. Rashida Tlaib spoke to a gathering of progressives and recounted a conversation with her young son. She quoted her son, saying, "Look, Mama, you won. Bullies don't win." And Tlaib responded by saying, "Baby, they don't, because we're gonna go in there and impeach the [expletive]."[14] Classy, these people I work with.

From Hateful Rhetoric to Violence

The breakdown in discourse today, and the hateful rhetoric we see, even from members of Congress, can be traced to the Alinsky tactics Obama popularized. Alinsky's style of speaking in terms of enemies and "polarization" has had a corrosive effect on political discourse. The rise of the violent group Antifa, short for anti-fascists, is the result of the Alinsky model of polarization.

Hannah Arendt, a philosopher who studied the methods of totalitarian regimes, identified the phenomenon preceding racism—"race-thinking."[15] In other words, before racism can take root, there must be a foundation where it becomes acceptable to think in terms of race, and to think of oneself and one's own race in opposition to other races. In the same way race-thinking is a precursor to racism, so, too, are Alinsky's "enemy-thinking" and violence rhetoric precursors to violent actions leveled against political enemies. Alinksy's heated language for labeling and "freezing" an enemy creates fertile ground for radical groups to act in violence.

Senator Ted Cruz of Texas has correctly called Antifa "a left-wing anarchist terrorist organization," calling for the Justice Department to investigate the rise in violent acts by the group.[16] Members who identify with Antifa are known for their habit of donning masks and engaging in brutal attacks on college campuses and at political events.

The radical group has engaged in attacks on an Immigration and a Customs Enforcement detention center in Tacoma, Washington, beating journalists and conservative speakers, and setting fire to cars. At a University of California at Berkeley event, Antifa members threw lit fireworks and bricks at police officers to protest a speech Milo Yiannopoulos, a conservative British political commentator, was delivering on campus.

Antifa has taken full credit for these activities, and promises on its social media sites it will commit more violent attacks.

Denigrating America

As a former college football player and high school football coach, I have a lifelong love for the sport. That's why I was so offended when the progressives used professional football to attack our identity as united Americans.

The football players who chose to kneel for the national anthem chose divisive identity politics over the American spirit of unity. In kneeling, those players demeaned not only our country and our flag, but also our shared identity as Americans.

The reaction to the NFL kneelers was swift and severe. An overwhelming number of Americans were outraged, and I was pleased to see people coming together in response. Our disgust at the NFL players' lack of respect for our country stemmed, in part, from our sense as Americans that our nation is not just worth rising for during the national anthem, but it is also worth laying down our lives for our country in wars.

The words from "America the Beautiful" again come to mind. In a lesser-known verse, we sing words honoring the men and women who have made the ultimate sacrifice to preserve our liberty. "Who more than self their country loved" and also, "When once or twice for man's avail, men lavished precious life!" Our nation is "America the beautiful" for more reasons than simply our gorgeous land stretching from sea to shining sea. Our nation has earned the label "beautiful" because of the unity connecting us to one another in this experiment to advance individual liberty. It is for that reason so many Americans have been willing to pay with their lives to ensure the continuation of this experiment.

Speaking of the challenges facing America, President Ronald Reagan, in his first inaugural address, in 1981, said, "It does require [...] our best effort, and our willingness to believe in ourselves and to believe in our capacity to perform great deeds; to believe that together, with God's help, we can and will resolve the problems which now confront us."[17] The word "together" is instructive. Reagan saw Americans' unity in approaching problems as our greatest strength. He closed his first speech as president with a characteristic display of optimism in the form of a rhetorical question. "And after all, why shouldn't we believe that? We are Americans."[18]

Indeed, we are!

CHAPTER 12

Tackling Problems the Right Way

"Americans believe their freedom to be the best instrument
and surest safeguard of their welfare: they are attached to the one
by the other."[1]

—ALEXIS DE TOCQUEVILLE

Barack Obama's presidency marked a dramatic departure from the founders' vision for our nation and individual freedom. He launched a new era of collectivist thinking through his agenda and his rhetoric. In his second inaugural address, his preference for the collective over the individual was on full display.

In that speech, Obama started with the familiar words from the Declaration of Independence: "We hold these truths to be self-evident, that all men are created equal, that they are endowed by their Creator with certain unalienable Rights, that among these are Life, Liberty, and the pursuit of Happiness."

He went on to assert, "fidelity to our founding principles requires new responses to new challenges; that preserving our individual freedom ultimately requires collective action."[2]

President Obama's reading of our nation's cherished founding documents led him to the flawed conclusion the "collective" is indispensable to individual liberty.

Obama's distortion of the clear text of the Declaration of Independence is representative of a trend we often see from the progressives; they rarely come right out and admit they are undermining the Constitution. President Obama was able to manipulate the language of individual liberty to find a call for collectivism. His misleading speech indicated collectivism is the extension of, rather than the rejection of, our heritage of individual liberty.

President Obama rooted his socialist call to action firmly within the familiar language of the Declaration of Independence because he knew his audience, the American people, would never go for an outright appeal for socialism, or for the wholesale rejection of our founding principles. This technique has been used by progressives for the last hundred years, and we should be able to recognize it.

Franklin Delano Roosevelt's Economic Bill of Rights, or "Second Bill of Rights" speech, was a similarly blatant attempt to co-opt the language of our founders. He even borrowed the "self-evident" expression from the Declaration of Independence, when he described "economic truths."[3] As justification for expanding the federal government, he said, "In our day these economic truths have become accepted as self-evident. We have accepted, so to speak, a second Bill of Rights under which a new basis of security and prosperity can be established for all regardless of station, race, or creed."[4] For progressives, the Constitution is inadequate. What is needed is an updated and collective-oriented Constitution.

Another progressive who mastered the art of manipulating the founders' words was Frank Goodnow, then president of Johns Hopkins University, who, in 1916, became the first president of the American Political Science Association. Speaking at Brown University, he spelled out his reasons for believing the founders over-emphasized the individual when they should have been emphasizing the collective. Again, though, he did not come right out and attack our nation's founding principles. Instead, he argued that we have moved beyond—or "progressed"—from the need for individual liberty. In his speech, he criticized the founders' emphasis on what he called "an extreme individualism."[5] He elaborated that our nation, in its founding, adopted "a doctrine of unadulterated individualism. Everyone had rights. Social duties were hardly recognized, or if recognized little emphasis was laid upon them."[6]

It is worth noting how he derided the foundational principle that every individual possessed rights, as an insufficient feature for a society that cherishes liberty. He inverted the individual liberty—and individual rights—to stress an invented notion of collective duty.

As we have seen, progressives—whether academic progressives or presidents such as Roosevelt and Obama—have provided clear examples of the wrong ways to approach problems. Their tactics invariably rely on the subordination of the individual in favor of collective solutions, ignoring or twisting the Constitution to support their agenda, and resorting to violent and divisive responses. The question for us, then, is how do we appropriately tackle the real problems facing our country?

Understand the Origin of Our Liberty

The best way to tackle our problems today is to steer clear of the progressives' false language of liberty. It is easy to be led down the wrong path and find ourselves agreeing with progressive solutions once we have bought into their flawed premises. The language the progressives use is intentionally steeped in just enough of our founding principles to be seductive to the American ear. Our republic requires that each generation commit to prioritizing individual liberty. It is not enough our forefathers had the genius idea to make the individual the central focus of our government; we must each understand what that means.

In his first State of the Union speech, George Washington conveyed the importance of teaching new generations what makes our nation great and free. He explained, the "security of a free Constitution" requires "teaching the people themselves to know and to value their own rights; to discern and provide against invasions of them," and to unite "a speedy, but temperate vigilance against encroachments, with an inviolable respect for the laws."[7]

Washington knew there would be those who would come along and encroach on our individual rights, and even provide justifications rooted in the familiar language of the Constitution. Without proper education in constitutional principles, Washington warned, we would be susceptible to arguments that the Constitution means something other than what it says.

One of my goals on each tour of the Capitol is to instill in my visitors a sense of our founders' prioritization of individual liberty. Many Americans today, thanks, in large part, to the progressives' rhetoric about the collective, are unclear why the individual must be the focus of our government. Isn't it more efficient to focus on the collective, what the group wants? Shouldn't the majority's needs be a larger priority than each individual's rights?

Frank S. Meyer, one of the founding editors of *National Review,* brilliantly explained in his book *In Defense of Freedom,* the reason why our rights are held at the individual level, not the collective level. The collective, coming together as a society, is an abstract concept. Our founders understood that our individual rights are "unalienable." Collectivists, by contrast, view individual rights as an extension of the collective's rights. If society is the primary entity in our political system, then society can revoke any rights the individual enjoys. Meyer put it this way: "…if society is an organism, the men who make it up can be no more than cells in the body of society; and society, not they, becomes the criterion by which moral and political matters are judged."[8] The problem, he said, is "…whatever 'rights' individual men may be allowed are pseudo rights, granted and revocable by society. The moral claims of the person are in effect reduced to nothingness."[9]

Reinstate Personal Responsibility

One of the most corrosive consequences of the progressives' insistence on the collective is the loss of individual responsibility. Personal responsibility is a unique aspect of the American character, and fittingly, the term came into circulation thanks to our founding fathers. The term "personal responsibility" came into circulation in 1787, and began to show up in various written records. In fact, the reason we keep a public record of senators' votes, and now House members' as well, is because Virginia delegate Edmund Randolph encouraged the practice to create a culture of "personal responsibility."

The notion of personal responsibility was a distinguishing feature of the new American government. In Federalist No. 69, Hamilton used the term "personal responsibility" to showcase one of the differences between the president of the new nation and the British king.[10] Unlike the king, the American president would be held to a different standard of personal responsibility because he would be elected.

Alexis de Tocqueville considered personal responsibility part of the American "character." In *Democracy in America,* he outlined the complicated relationship between the private citizen's actions and the common welfare. "An American attends to his private concerns as if he were alone in the world, and the next minute he gives himself up to the common welfare as if he had forgotten them.... The inhabitants of the United States alternately display so strong and so similar a passion for their own welfare and for their freedom that it may be supposed that these passions are united and mingled in some part of their character."[11]

De Tocqueville captured an essential element of our character that endures today: our abiding belief, as Americans, in personal responsibility. It's that sense of individual responsibility that resides at the core of the debate over abortion. The Left will have you believe abortion is about a "right," when it is fundamentally about killing an unborn child. Progressives remove the language of personal responsibility from the debate; it's not a human being, they say. It's a fetus. It's not about an unwanted pregnancy; it's about a right to do what you want with your body. With abortion "rights," the left has co-opted the language of liberty, putting forth the notion it's a woman's right to choose, that it's about the collective. But what about the most important person in this entire equation—the baby, who, they would have us believe, has no rights? Bill Clinton, when he was president, talked the language of the Left, speaking about abortion being safe, legal, and rare—a poor attempt of a liberal politician trying to assuage the fears of Americans, as if he were trying to say, *We're not promoting abortions in this country*. Never mind that abortion has gone in a different direction since then—not so safe, nor so rare.

I've been a prosecutor for most of my professional life. I have always believed my duty was to give voice to victims in a courtroom. To advocate on their behalf. Now that I'm in public office, I believe one of my essential duties is to give voice to the unborn. They don't have a voice. They can't speak for themselves. My faith compels me, and my past experience as a prosecutor instructs me to be an advocate for the unborn. Just consider Proverbs 31:8-10: "Speak up for those who cannot speak for themselves, for the rights of all who are destitute. Speak up and judge fairly; defend the rights of the poor and needy."

This was the message of Jesus, who embraced lepers and other outcasts. And I say we should heed that call—elected leaders and citizens alike—to find a moral cause, to know right from wrong, to speak out when the occasion arises, and to do the right thing.

* * *

Sometimes, the better course of action is to speak less, which is certainly the case with Massachusetts Senator Elizabeth Warren. Borrowing from the progressive playbook, she has talked a lot about erasing college debt for everyone. The collective will take on the burden of the cost, by her way of thinking. Lost in the calculation is the loss of personal investment in one's own education—and personal responsibility. In conversations with me, several Colorado University presidents have expressed opposition to the idea of a free college education for all. Why? Because nothing is free. As soon as the federal government makes college education free, these university presidents fear , the collective will start telling you what the college bathrooms should look like and what curriculum you have to teach. It's a bad trade: A so-called free education in exchange for the government's control over our children until they graduate from college. There is, of course, the inherent unfairness in the trade as well: Why should someone who doesn't go to college have to help pay for someone who does? The right solution resides in the private marketplace, where people are responsible for their own education. It's a simple equation: individual responsibility equals individual benefit.

What is equally true is the loss of individual responsibility can foster trouble. That's where Antifa, the violent leftist group, comes in. They operate in groups, often with masks, hiding their identity in the collective. Such was the case on Halloween 2019, when a group of six masked men approached the door of Andy Ngo, the conservative journalist. The men wore masks with printouts of Ngo's face. They pounded on his window and made him fear for his safety. None carried trick-or-treat bags.

"This is the latest addition to a long list of Antifa-related individuals doxing, threatening, and promising to hurt or kill me or my family," Ngo wrote in a statement, then.

It's also just one example of thugs, whose identities are masked, operating in the anonymity of the collective, feeling empowered to threaten, to get away with things, with no real consequences. Earlier that summer, Ngo had been attacked, hospitalized, and left with internal head bleeding after a confrontation with leftist protestors in Portland. "I was beaten on the head & robbed on 29 June," Ngo tweeted. "Antifa then continued to hurl 'milk-shakes' at my bleeding face. I was hospitalized with a brain hemorrhage. There still hasn't been a single arrest by @PortlandPolice."

This isn't the America contemplated by our founding fathers. They saw the risks of the mob. What the founders hoped for is what we need to return to: Communities need to start coming together, holding people responsible. We need more neighborhood policing. We need more police on foot, instead of patrol cars, building relationships. We cannot allow thugs to take away our rights, to threaten our communities. We need to promote individual rights more. Think about it. The more we are allowed to keep the profits of our hard work, the more generous we become, the more attached we are to our community, the more charitable we are.

This is, of course, the opposite of what happens to the collective in a repressive socialist society where, famously, the saying goes, if you're waiting in line for a loaf of bread, you're not plotting to overthrow the government. That's the dynamic in socialist countries, where they seek to secure the welfare of the nation first, before the freedom of the individual. For us, personal welfare is secured by individual rights. It's the American way, as understood by de Tocqueville, who said, "And indeed the Americans believe their freedom to be the best instrument and surest safeguard of their welfare; they are attached to the one by the other."[12]

Reject the Divisiveness

I also like to point out a reminder of our Constitution's ability to be amended: a statue of suffragists who ushered in the right for women to vote, as granted through the Nineteenth Amendment. The statue is an eight-ton block of unfinished marble.

It is a unique statue near the brown metal statue of Ronald Reagan, in the rotunda of the Capitol. All the other statues in the Capitol depict a single individual. This statue, however, memorializes three women, all nineteenth-century Republicans, all abolitionists, all temperance supporters, and all leaders of the suffragist movement. In addition to depicting multiple images, this statue is distinctive because it is partially unfinished.

The busts of leading suffragettes Susan B. Anthony, Lucrieta Mott, and Elizabeth Cady Stanton were prominently displayed at the Chicago World's Exposition, in 1893. The National Women's Party chose the sculptor of those three busts, Abigail Johnson, to create a memorial for the ratification of the Nineteenth Amendment, giving women the right to vote. The unveiling ceremony took place in the Capitol rotunda, on February 15th, 1921, the 101st anniversary of Susan B. Anthony's birth.

In the upper left-hand corner of the statue, there is an unfinished marble block, as if Johnson intended that a future woman's image should appear to finish her work. No written record exists of Johnson's vision, but several historians have speculated the artist intended that the memorial should be finished with a bust of the first woman president of the United States. Many progressives believed, heading into the 2016 election, Hillary Rodham Clinton's image would appear on the memorial.

That disappointment, combined with the reality that progressives would not be able to solidify the gains they made under President Obama, caused one of the most divisive times in our country's history. Every time my progressive colleagues walk from the Speaker's office to the House floor to vote, they pass the unfinished image on the women's suffrage memorial, and they are reminded how their quest to transform America was interrupted by Donald Trump's successful presidential campaign. And I'm sure they seethe with animosity. After all, they are smarter than the rest of us; they know what we need better than we do.

At the same time progressives push for collective action and collectivist approaches to our rights, they have created a divisive us-vs-them vitriolic culture. Here, the relationship between John Adams and Thomas Jefferson is instructive. Theirs was among the most famous American friendships in constant feud. From the beginning, the two men stood on opposite sides of the political spectrum of the new nation—Adams advocating for a strong national government, while Jefferson called for states' rights. In the Capitol, the famous painting of the Declaration of Independence seems to give a nod to that feud, with Jefferson appearing to be stepping on Adams's foot.

Tensions began to arise when Adams served as vice president to George Washington, while Jefferson served as secretary of state. Things only got worse when Washington declined to run a third time, and Adams and Jefferson ran against each other to fill the presidential void. Adams barely won, and Jefferson refused to serve as vice president, as was then the constitutional mandate. But Jefferson got his revenge, beating Adams for president the next time around. They didn't speak to each other for the next twelve years.

In 1812, though, a mutual friend encouraged the two rivals to write letters to each other, and thus was born an uneasy friendship that blossomed before yielding nearly two hundred missives. "You and I ought not to die before we have explained ourselves to each other," Adams wrote, early on to Jefferson.[13] The latter took the suggestion to heart, and the tense relationship between the two former presidents eased, as both recognized they could be rivals in the marketplace of ideas, while maintaining respect for one another.

Perhaps it was divine providence, but on the fiftieth anniversary of the Declaration of Independence—July 4, 1826—the two former presidents died within hours of each other. Unfortunately, the way they honored the right to disagree agreeably has died of late, as progressives have succumbed to drowning out what they don't like, with venomous language of hatred.

The Liberty Reminders

After leading tours of the Capitol, I often engage in discussions with my visitors about practical applications for everything we saw. Through those discussions, I have developed a call to action, a handy reminder for individuals and families to help keep our nation on track, firmly rooted in liberty.

For instance, I will ask my visitors if their schools still pledge allegiance to our flag. Progressives have worked hard to remove the Pledge of Allegiance from our schools, and they don't want to stop there in their attempt to wrest control of the educational system. So I ask, what else is your school doing? Be inquisitive. Get involved. Ask your children if they understand the difference between a republic and democracy. Find out how your children's teachers are evaluated.

When my son was in elementary school, his third-grade science teacher was horrible; he never assigned homework, he didn't care, he let the kids watch movies in class. So I went to the principal, asking whether the school had ever considered getting rid of this teacher. The principal said it was difficult to get rid of any teacher, but she assured me there was an unspoken policy that no two children from the same family would be subjected to that teacher.

We need to do better. We need to demand more of our schools. And we need to fight against the slide, the abdication of personal responsibility in the local school systems. In 2019, for instance, the Colorado legislature passed an educational mandate requiring third graders to learn about and accept abortion. The bill, as it turned out, was written by Planned Parenthood. More shockingly, the measure applies not only to public schools, but to private schools and home schoolers—and it spread like a virus to several other states.

* * *

For individuals, my liberty reminders include that our founders built in a unique feature of our system—the right to petition our government for policy changes. The open structure of the Capitol is an invitation for all Americans to exercise their First Amendment right to petition the government. I, for one, take this seriously. I read my constituents' emails. I get on the phone with them. I care what they think. And I say we should all engage in meaningful discourse; not just our elected leaders, but the electorate as well. We need to converse in the tradition of Jefferson and Adams—with civility. In the age of social media, we have to resist the shout-out culture of Facebook and Twitter. We've all seen the breakdown in decorum online. It's the way it works on the web; people will send you something nasty they would never dare say to your face. We have to resist this kind of behavior. The breakdown in communication on an individual level affects us on a broader level, as a community, as a state, as a nation. We don't advance dialogue in our country with vicious verbal attacks. That's why I didn't support my Republican colleagues' attempt to censure Adam Schiff, the Democrat who chaired the House Intelligence Committee in October 2019. While it's true Schiff's conduct was woeful in connection to the impeachment proceedings, I didn't feel Schiff's actions rose to the level of a censure.

Historically, that measure has been reserved for more severe and rare conduct—primarily, criminal conduct. I felt Schiff should have apologized. But I was eviscerated by some conservatives in Colorado, who used colorful language to castigate me. This is what I say: Go ahead and criticize me if you like. But let's be grown up about it. Let's agree to disagree and do so agreeably.

Besides, we can't let the hate drown out the debate, especially about matters of importance. We need to focus on the questions, not the noise. For instance, does a candidate running for office believe the Electoral College is worth preserving? Does the candidate believe the right to bear arms is an individual right?

And how about getting involved in the political process? Join a recreation board, apply to serve on a water board, get appointed to a retention board for judges. If you get involved, you can have an impact on the community. Volunteer to work on campaigns, bring your kids along, teach them how elections in your state work. When I had a real job, as a prosecutor, I brought my daughter to work. How many people take their kids to the ballot box to see how our system of governance works, to understand the importance of voting?

We expect a lot of newcomers to America, when they apply for U.S. citizenship, to care about supporting and defending the Constitution. About staying informed on issues affecting their community. About participating in the democratic process. About respecting and obeying federal, state, and local laws. About respecting the rights, beliefs, and opinions of others. About participating in their local community. About paying their taxes honestly. About serving on a jury when called on. About defending our great country, if needed.

What we expect of newcomers, we should expect of all Americans. And what we might take for granted, whether it's our individual prosperity or that of our great nation, I say we should offer heartfelt thanks. I'm reminded of President Lincoln's Thanksgiving proclamation, in 1863. Back then, Thanksgiving was celebrated at different times in different states. That is, until seventy-four-year-old Sarah Josepha Hale wrote a letter to the president, urging him to affix a national day of thanksgiving. Hale clamored for such a day for fifteen years. Lincoln ended that striving, announcing on October 3, 1863, that going forward, we as nation would pause as one, in thanksgiving.

"The year that is drawing towards its close has been filled with the blessings of fruitful fields and healthful skies," President Lincoln began. "To these bounties, which are so constantly enjoyed that we are prone to forget the source from which they come, others have been added, which are of so extraordinary a nature, that they cannot fail to penetrate and soften even the heart which is habitually insensible to the ever watchful providence of Almighty God."[14]

Amen.

Conclusion

> "[W]hile democracy seeks equality in liberty, socialism seeks equality in restraint and servitude."[1]
>
> —ALEXIS DE TOCQUEVILLE

On the morning of September 11, 2001, as the hijacker terrorists made their final arrangements for the deadly attacks, both the House and the Senate were in session. First Lady Laura Bush was in the Russell Senate Office Building, preparing to speak to the Senate HELP Committee, on education matters. Federal investigators believe United Flight 93, the hijacked plane that crashed in Somerset County, Pennsylvania, was heading toward the Capitol building before passengers and crew attempted to regain control of the plane. The tragic possibility that our sorrows could have been compounded with a successful attack on the Capitol dome is a reminder of the significance of the Capitol building and it being the very symbol of our freedom.

Everywhere we look, while we tour the Capitol, we see symbolism harkening back to the classical world—ancient Greece and Rome. Some aspects are easier to recognize than others. Certainly, the pillars in the crypt, the arches near the old Senate Chamber, and the style of the old Supreme Court Chamber evoke images of the ancient world.

Less obvious perhaps is the Capitol sitting on a hill, as did the legislative houses in Rome and Greece. The term "Senate," comes from the state councils of Rome. Our word for someone who runs for office, "candidate," is derived from the Latin, *candidatus*, which denoted a person running for office in ancient Rome. The Mace of the House of Representatives is

173

an emblem of ancient Roman authority. It was an ancient battle weapon, similar to the fasces, a bundle of rods with an axe blade, that were used by kings and consuls to signify strength through unity. *E pluribus Unum* on display again.

The classical art, architecture, and traditions in the Capitol are important beyond their aesthetic beauty because they symbolize tradition and its continued relevance in maintaining the political process in a free society. Our founders studied and learned from ancient philosophy, and traditions and sought to build a republic from those lessons.

Tradition is significant in the American experience. It's one of the reasons why America is fundamentally conservative. It's why progressives have to destroy tradition to implement their agenda. As just one example, progressives argue that the Constitution is a living document and should not be interpreted literally.

The Romans promoted the concept of tradition when they adopted Greek thought and culture and made it their own. With the Romans, tradition became a guide for future behavior. It signaled to future generations what was and was not important. It was the thread running through the past, present, and future. And most importantly, it conveyed authority.

When viewed from the perspective of tradition and authority, the challenges of the modern world—that is, maintaining natural individual rights and avoiding their degradation by adopting popular and temporary collective rights—are more clearly seen. The American revolution was different because it was a revolution that affirmed history and tradition and the authority it conveyed rather than destroyed it, like the French and Russian revolutions. The American Revolution, in contrast to other revolutions, was undertaken not to create an entirely new political system, but rather to codify existing political structures and agreements, including the state charters. We can take pride and laugh about the uniqueness of the American experience—even in our revolutions, we are conservative.

In the United States, authority resides in the people and is expressed in the Constitution. In 1796, James Madison acknowledged this relationship between popular authority and the Constitution, arguing that, prior to its ratification, the Constitution "was nothing more than the draught of a plan, nothing but a dead letter until life and validity were breathed into it, by the voice of the people."[2]

By virtue of this authority, the Constitution gives the government its power, and stipulates the ways in which that power may be used and the ends to which it may be directed. The Constitution and our electoral system also provide the means by which the people can check the government when it abuses its power.

In the American context, the Constitution's institutions make political conflict legitimate. Taken together, they create the space where the people and their elected representatives can peacefully resolve their differences. By engaging in politics, Americans affirm their fidelity to the Constitution's authority and its institutions as instruments of legitimate political rule.

In today's America, progressives seek to obscure tradition, and many Americans no longer understand the history and value of our traditions. This is a problem because, as Russell Kirk put it, "True progress, improvement, is unthinkable without tradition…because progress rests upon addition, not subtraction."[3] Edmund Burke understood well what happened when a people forgot their tradition. He wrote, in *Reflections on the Revolution in France*, "When ancient opinions and rules of life are taken away, the loss cannot possibly be estimated. From that moment we have no compass to govern us, nor can we know distinctly to what port we steer."[4]

Our founders, and their contemporaries, held a deep interest in what a freedom-advancing future could entail. Their interest in the future was equally matched by their interest in the past. They studied history, not just political and legal philosophy. The founders possessed a fascination with the Greek and Roman empires, and they paid attention to what had worked in those political systems. But they also paid attention to what didn't work. Why did those political systems collapse?

Their reading selections, including Edward Gibbon's masterpiece, *The History of the Decline and Fall of the Roman Empire*, make clear the founders and other early Americans were committed to avoiding the pitfalls of past political systems because they knew this experiment was not an easy one.

Our challenge today is to conduct a similar study of the examples of failed political systems. Communism and socialism have failed across the globe, and Karl Marx's predictions have each proven false. Our best defense against the seductive promises of socialism is a well-informed public, fully aware of the inevitable destruction socialism produces. Promises of free giveaways are the easy route. Committing ourselves to teaching our children and grandchildren about the evils of socialism, and the progress achieved under republican capitalism, is a far harder option. But it's the route our founders would expect us to take.

There was a time when it seemed impossible for the Greek empire to ever be eclipsed. There was also a time in history when no one could have conceived of the powerful Roman empire falling. Today, we cannot imagine a time when the United States of America won't exist. But Daniel Webster, speaking before the New York Historical Society, in 1852, warned of that possibility: "...no man can tell, how sudden a catastrophe may overwhelm us, that shall bury all our glory in profound obscurity."[5]

What could cause such a calamity? According to Webster, our collapse from greatness would happen if we allow anything to "recklessly destroy the political constitution."[6] That political constitution is more than simply our written Constitution. It is also the tradition that creates the fabric of our identity as Americans—our identity as hard workers who embrace challenges.

The primary threat to our great republic today comes from the progressives' agenda and false promises of an easy future paved with free gifts from the government. If progressives like Franklin Delano Roosevelt conceived of the original nanny state, the progressives have modernized the concept, with the government now portrayed as an excessively indulgent and hyper-involved helicopter parent.

Friedrich Hayek explained in *The Road to Serfdom,* why the progressives are forced to resort to these promises of a "new freedom," whether "economic security" or freedom from fear, or freedom from student debts. They cloak their agenda of big government programs in the language of "new freedom" because Americans are naturally suspicious of larger government and socialist programs.[7]

Recognizing that socialism was unpalatable to most Americans because it was associated with "restraint and servitude,"[8] to use a phrase from de Tocqueville, the early progressives instead co-opted our language of liberty. They were advancing socialism, they claimed, as a way to enhance freedom. Their agenda would usher in "freedom from want,"[9] and today we hear the echoes of this freedom promise in the progressive candidates' platforms. The freedom from the burden of student debt. Freedom from fear of not having health insurance. Freedom that comes from knowing the government will pay for your birth control pills.

The progressives' control agenda has taken on even more extreme forms in recent years. In 2012, New York City's mayor Michael Bloomberg proposed a limit on the size of soft drinks in the city. The rule went into effect in 2013, and remained in effect until the New York Court of Appeals ruled that this regulation greatly exceed the New York City Board of Health's authority.[10] It is an important reminder that a government big enough to dictate the size of your soft drink is a government big enough to take away everything you have, and to do just about anything in the private sphere. What could possibly be off limits at that point?

There is no such thing as a free lunch, and that is even more true when it comes to the government. The government can give to one group, but only by taking from another group. Those gifts bestowed on certain people come from taking property, or opportunities, or higher taxes from other Americans. The progressives demonstrate a strident selfishness. *My* needs matter more than anyone else's rights.

We see that blind selfishness on a larger scale as well, with the national debt. Progressives are not simply content to take from their fellow contemporary Americans. They are equally comfortable, or perhaps even more comfortable, taking from future generations. The national debt we continue to rack up is a form of generational socialism. We are seizing property from future generations to satisfy our wants today.

The founders correctly understood, our nation's liberty experiment would quickly come to an end if we institutionalized the practice of borrowing from future generations without regard for their welfare, and Madison believed that was particularly true if future generations were forced to finance past generations' wars. In an op-ed in *National Gazette*, on February 2, 1792, Madison explained the risk posed by this type of borrowing. "Each generation should be made to bear the burden of its own wars, instead of carrying them on, at the expense of other generations."

Forcing each generation to pay for its own wars would have the immediate effect of returning the war-making authority back to the people, through our representatives in Congress. The authority to authorize war, which rightfully belongs to Congress, takes on an even sharper meaning in light of Madison's caution.

The progressives' language inverts the wisdom of the founders. The plain text of the Bill of Rights provides great insight here. The founders knew the government could never function as a benevolent granter of wishes. They understood the inevitable tendency of governments to take from individuals. The Bill of Rights is worded carefully to reflect the danger that government would take away God-granted rights. The First Amendment, therefore, says, "Congress shall make no law respecting an establishment of religion, or prohibiting the free exercise thereof; or abridging the freedom of speech, or of the press; or the right of the people peaceably to assemble, and to petition the Government for a redress of grievances." With one amendment, we see six restrictions placed on the government.

Progressives today, rather than carrying out the founders' vision for a government held in check by the people, are promising ever bigger government to meet the day-to-day wants of every citizen. A republic, if we can keep it, cannot be held together with the promises of free gifts granted to certain groups of people, at the expense of other groups, even future generations.

We are at a crossroads today and we have a choice to make. The choice is between the easy path, as portrayed by the progressives, or the harder option of following tradition, respecting authority, and resisting the urge to take the free stuff, with its accompanying restrictions on our God-given freedoms.

It is easy to curtail freedom of speech, and silence the opinions we dislike. It is far more difficult to commit to a culture, whether on a college campus or on social media, that respects other opinions and engages in civil discourse.

Similarly, it is easy to get caught up in the progressives' anti-gun hysteria and buy into their gun-restricting agenda. It is harder to commit to upholding the Second Amendment and to teaching younger generations about the necessity of responsible gun ownership as a method of "self-preservation," to use Jefferson's term, as self-defense in our neighborhoods and as the ultimate barrier against a would-be tyrannical government. Even better will be to train this generation and future generations to respect all lives as unique creations of God. Taking of innocent human life will be judged by the Creator.

Progressives trust government to solve all our problems and to stop crime, even though government has proven woefully inadequate in this area. The central question in the gun control debate is: Do you trust law-abiding individuals to play a part in their own protection, or do you believe it is exclusively the job of the government to defend our homes?

Political correctness is the greatest threat to freedom of speech, and our challenge is to resist the easy path of allowing the progressives' nation-wide sensitivity training to trample on our right to speak our minds. We have a choice to make, and there is no middle-ground compromise: Do we cherish the God-given right to exercise free speech, or do we want every individual, in every profession, to be forced to abide by the progressives' political correctness?

These aren't easy questions, but neither are they avoidable.

The progressives' retrograde ideas cause the type of social upheaval the founders tried to avoid. With the growth in the federal government, expansion of the bureaucracy, increase in judicial activism, coupled with the decline of federalism, deterioration of free speech, we see the decay of a moral society. The objective measurements stare at us from every corner of the country; single-parent families, high crime rates, mass incarceration, lower educational standards, less patriotism, and disrespect for police.

On Capitol tours, I often ask if anyone has ever visited the Coliseum in Rome or the Parthenon in Athens, and I ask what the difference is between our Capitol and those historic sites.

The difference is we go to Rome and Athens to view ruins of once-great civilizations, and wonder about what could have been. We come to the Capitol, on the other hand, to marvel at how far we have come as a nation, and wonder about what the future might hold.

The Capitol invites us to study our nation's history of advancing individual liberty, and to then commit ourselves to doing the hard work necessary to keep our republic.

Endnotes

INTRODUCTION

1 Patrick Henry, Speech, Virginia Convention, March 23, 1775, George Carruth and Eugene Ehrlich, "The Harper Book of American Quotations," (New York: A Hudson Group Book, Wing Books, 1994), 273.

2 "From John Adams to John Taylor, 17 December 1814," *Founders Online,* National Archives, https://founders.archives.gov/documents/Adams/99-02-02-6371.

CHAPTER 1

1 Ronald Reagan, "First Inaugural Address," Speech, Washington, D.C., January 20, 1981, https://www.reaganfoundation.org/media/128614/inaguration.pdf.

2 Alexander Hamilton, "Federalist No.1," in *The Federalist Papers,* ed. Clinton Rossiter (New York: New American Library, 1961), 1.

3 James Madison, "Federalist No. 43," in *The Federalist Papers,* ed. Clinton Rossiter (New York: New American Library, 1961), 240.

4 Elizabeth Kite, L'Enfant and Washington, 1791-1792: Published and Unpublished Documents Now Brought Together for the First Time, June 10, 1783, in Elizabeth Kite, L'Enfant and Washington, 1791-1792 Published and Unpublished Documents Now Brought Together for the First Time (Baltimore: Johns Hopkins University Press, 1929), 62–67.

5 Edmund Burke, "Speech on Conciliation with the Colonies," March 22, 1775, Philip B. Kurland and Ralph Lerner, eds., *The Founders' Constitution,* Vol. 1, Fundamental Documents, Document 2 (Chicago: The University of Chicago Press, 1986), 6.

6 Mark A. Mastromarino, ed., The Papers of George Washington, Presidential Series, vol. 9, 23 September 1791–29 February 1792 (Charlottesville: University Press of Virginia, 2000), 244.

7 Ronald Reagan, "Remarks on East-West Relations at the Brandenburg Gate in West Berlin," June 12, 1987., Available at: https://www.reaganfoundation.org/media/128814/brandenburg.pdf.

8 Ronald Reagan, "America's Best Days Are Yet to Come," Speech, Republican National Convention, August 17, 1992., Available at: https://www.chicagotribune.com/news/ct-xpm-1992-08-18-9203150298-story.html.

9 Ronald Reagan, "First Inaugural Address," Washington, D.C., January 20, 1981., Available at: https://www.reaganfoundation.org/media/128614/inaguration.pdf.

10 Barack Obama, Press Conference, Palaiz de la Musique et Des Congres, Stras-
    bourg, France, April 4, 2009., Available at: https://obamawhitehouse.archives.gov/
    the-press-office/news-conference-president-obama-4042009.

11 Alexandria Ocasio-Cortez, Interview, "Firing Line," July 16, 2018., Available at:
    https://www.dailywire.com/news/watch-ocasio-cortez-explains-unemployment-melts
    -james-barrett.

12 Barack Obama, Speech, Chicago, Illinois, April 28, 2010. Available at: https://www.
    realclearpolitics.com/video/2010/04/28/obama_to_wall_street_i_do_think_at_a_
    certain_point_youve_made_enough_money.html.

13 Barack Obama, Campaign speech, July 13, 2012. Available at:, https://www.wsj.com/
    articles/SB10001424052702304388004577533300916053684.

14 James Madison, "Property," The Papers of James Madison, ed. W.T. Hutchinson et al.
    (Chicago and London: University of Chicago Press), 1962–1977 (vols. 1–10), 14:266–268.

CHAPTER 2

1 James Madison, "Federalist No. 51," in *The Federalist Papers*, ed. Clinton Rossiter (New
   York: New American Library, 1961), 290.

2 L'Enfant's explanation of the plan, in Elizabeth Kite, L'Enfant and Washington, 1791–
   1792 Published and Unpublished Documents Now Brought Together for the First Time
   (Baltimore: Johns Hopkins University Press, 1929), 62--67.

3 Pierre L'Enfant, Letter to President George Washington. Quoted by Architect of the
   Capitol., https://www.aoc.gov/history/capitol-hill.

4 James Madison, "Federalist No. 51," in *The Federalist Papers*, ed. Clinton Rossiter (New
   York: New American Library, 1961), 290.

5 Alexander Hamilton, Remarks, New York Ratifying Convention, Poughkeepsie, New
   York, June 27, 1788., https://founders.archives.gov/documents/Hamilton/01-05-02
   -0012-0034#ARHN-01-05-02-0012-0034-fn-0001.

6 James Madison, "Federalist No. 39," in *The Federalist Papers*, ed. Clinton Rossiter (New
   York: New American Library, 1961), 209.

7 James Wilson, Of the Study of Law in the United States, 1790–1792., http://founding
   .com/founders-library/american-political-figures/james-wilson/of-the-study-of-law
   -in-the-united-states/.

8 Donovan Slack, "Hillary Clinton Condemns Benghazi Attack," Politico, September 12,
   2012., https://www.politico.com/blogs/politico44/2012/09/hillary-clinton-condemns
   -benghazi-attack-135265.

9 Daniel Halper and Marisa Schultz, "Benghazi Report Shows Clinton Pushed Own
   Version of Attack," *New York Post*, June 28, 2016., https://nypost.com/2016/06/28/final
   -benghazi-report-blames-clinton-disregarding-witnesses/.

10 Anne Gearan, "Latest State Release: Clinton Emails with Chelsea after Benghazi Attacks
    and More," *The Washington Post*, January 8, 2016., https://www.washingtonpost.com/
    news/post-politics/wp/2016/01/08/with-2-a-m-state-department-email-trove-82-per-
    cent-of-clinton-emails-now-released/.

11 Stephen F. Hayes, "The Benghazi Lie in Black and White," Washington Examiner, June
    28, 2016,. https://www.washingtonexaminer.com/weekly-standard/the-benghazi-lie-in
    -black-and-white.

12 Ibid.

13 James Taranto, "What Difference Does It Make?," *The Wall Street Journal*, January 23, 2013., https://www.wsj.com/articles/SB1000142412788732353980457826000104467 4348.
14 George Mason, Remarks, Federal Convention, August 7, 1787, quoted in M. Farrand, The Records of the Federal Convention of 1787, vol. 2, 1911., https://oll.libertyfund. org/titles/farrand-the-records-of-the-federal-convention-of-1787-vol-2.

CHAPTER 3

1 James Madison, "Federalist No. 51," in *The Federalist Papers*, ed. Clinton Rossiter (New York: New American Library, 1961), 291.
2 30 Alexander Hamilton, "Examination Number 1," December 17, 1801., https://found-ers.archives.gov/documents/Hamilton/01-25-02-0264-0002.
3 Alexander Hamilton, "Federalist No. 34," *The Federalist Papers*, ed. Clinton Rossiter (New York: New American Library, 1961), 176–177.
4 Ken Buck, Public statement on the formation of the Bipartisan War Powers Working Group, https://khanna.house.gov/media/in-the-news/war-powers-back-congress-or -back-war.
5 Abraham Lincoln, Letter, quoted in M. Cuomo and H. Holzer, *Lincoln on Democracy*, (New York: Fordham University Press, 2004), pp. 36–37.
6 John Trumball, *Autobiography, Reminiscences and Letters of John Trumball from 1756 to 1841*, (New Haven: B.L. Hamlen, 1841), 429–430.

CHAPTER 4

1 James Madison, Speech in Virginia Convention, December 2, 1829, https://rotunda. upress.virginia.edu/founders/default.xqy?keys=FOEA-print-02-02-02-1924.
2 Carl Huse, "Executive Branch Overreach: Lawmakers Blame Themselves," *The New York Times,* February 8, 2016.
3 Ericka Andersen, "WATCH: Obama's Speechwriters Laugh at 'If You Like Your Plan, You Can Keep It' Lie," *National Review Online,* May 11, 2016, https://www.nationalre-view.com/corner/barack-obama-obamacare-plan-hilarious/.
4 David Harsanyi, "Obama's Legacy Will Be Executive Overreach," *The Federalist*, January 5, 2016, https://thefederalist.com/2016/01/05/obamas-legacy-will-be-executive-abuse/.
5 Burton W. Folsom, "The Progressive Income Tax in U.S. History," Foundation for Economic Education, May 1, 2003, https://fee.org/articles/the-progressive-income-tax -in-us-history/.
6 David Pietrusza, "'A Standard of Righteousness': The Worldview of Calvin Coolidge," Speech Delivered at 2010 JFK Symposium, https://www.coolidgefoundation.org/ resources/2010-jfk-symposium-3/.
7 Ed Driscoll, "Interview: Amity Shlaes Discusses Coolidge," PJ Media, February 11, 2013, https://pjmedia.com/eddriscoll/2013/2/11/amity-shlaes-coolidge-interview/.

CHAPTER 5

1 Charles Louis de Secondat, Baron de Montesquieu, *The Complete Works of M. de Montesquieu* (London: T. Evans, 1777), Vol. 1, 1/31/2020, https://oll.libertyfund.org/ titles/837.
2 "Building History," The Supreme Court of the United States, https://www.supreme-court.gov/about/buildinghistory.aspx.

3 Alexander Hamilton, "Federalist No. 78," *The Federalist Papers*, ed. Clinton Rossiter (New York: New American Library, 1961), 433–434.

4 Ibid., 433.

5 Charles Louis de Secondat, Baron de Montesquieu, *The Complete Works of M. de Montesquieu* (London: T. Evans, 1777), Vol. 1, 1/31/2020, https://oll.libertyfund.org/titles/837.

6 Marbury v. Madison 5 U.S. 137 (1803).

7 Thomas Jefferson, "Letter to Spencer Roane," September 6, 1819, in *The Works of Thomas Jefferson*. Collected and edited by Paul Leicester Ford. Federal Edition. 12 vols. New York and London: G. P. Putnam's Sons, 1904–5.

8 Ed Whelan, "On Originalism and Judicial Supremacy, Part 2," *National Review Online*, June 2, 2015, https://www.nationalreview.com/bench-memos/originalism-and-judicial-supremacy-part-2-ed-whelan/.

9 Woodrow Wilson, *Congressional Government: A Study in American Politics* (Boston: Houghton Mifflin Company: The Riverside Press Company, 1885).

10 Andrew Glass, "This Day in Politics: FDR Unveils 'Court-Packing' Plan, February 5, 1937," *Politico*, February 5, 2019, https://www.politico.com/story/2019/02/05/fdr-court-packing-1937-1144296.

11 "Developments in the Law—More Data, More Problems," 131 *Harv. L. Rev.* 1715, 1722 (2018).

12 Stephen Dinan, "Kavanaugh Accuser Admits to Making up Rape Accusation As 'Tactic,'" *The Associated Press*, November 4, 2018.

CHAPTER 6

1 Lord Acton, quoted in F.A. Hayek, *The Road to Serfdom*, (Chicago: The University of Chicago Press, 1994), 240.

2 James Madison, "Federalist No. 45," *The Federalist Papers*, ed. Clinton Rossiter (New York: New American Library, 1961), 260.

3 Thomas Jefferson, Letter to Charles Hammond, August 18, 1821, https://founders.archives.gov/documents/Jefferson/98-01-02-2260.

4 Kevin A. Carson, "Taylorism, Progressivism, and Rule by Experts," *The New Republic*, August 24, 2011, https://fee.org/articles/taylorism-progressivism-and-rule-by-experts/.

5 Thomas Sowell, "The Progressive Legacy," *National Review Online*, February 14, 2012, https://www.nationalreview.com/2012/02/progressive-legacy-thomas-sowell/.

6 "Historical Debt Outstanding – Annual 1900 – 1949," Treasury Direct, Accessed March 9, 2020, https://www.treasurydirect.gov/govt/reports/pd/histdebt/histdebt_histo3.htm.

7 Allen G. Breed, "'Poster Father' Weary of Sour Fate: Kentucky: Tom Fletcher Still Lives in the Hillside House Where Lyndon Johnson Visited. He Voices Resentment over Media Interest in His Life Story, in Which Most Luck Has Been Bad," *Associated Press*, June 26, 1994, https://www.latimes.com/archives/la-xpm-1994-06-26-mn-8651-story.html.

8 Ian Millhiser, "The Supreme Court Will Decide If 'Faithless Electors' Can Ignore the Will of the People," Vox, January 22, 2020, https://www.vox.com/policy-and-politics/2020/1/22/21074453/supreme-court-faithless-electors-chiafalo-baca.

9 "Supreme Court Asked to Decide If Electoral College Voters Are Bound to the State's Winner," CNN Wire, October 8, 2019, https://wreg.com/2019/10/08/

supreme-court-asked-to-decide-if-electoral-college-voters-are-bound-to-the-states-winner/.

CHAPTER 7

1 Frederick Douglass, "Plea for Free Speech in Boston," Boston, MA, December 9, 1880, https://frederickdouglass.infoset.io/islandora/object/islandora:2129#page/1/mode/1up.

2 Silence Dogood, No. 8, *The New England Courant*, July 9, 1722.

3 James Madison, "Public Opinion," *National Gazette*, December 19, 1791, https://founders.archives.gov/documents/Madison/01-14-02-0145.

4 Frederick Douglass, "Plea for Free Speech in Boston," Boston, MA, December 9, 1880, https://frederickdouglass.infoset.io/islandora/object/islandora:2129#page/1/mode/1up.

5 Robert Gillette, "Reagan Meets 96 Soviet Dissidents: He Praises Their Courage, Says, 'I Came to Give You Strength,'" *Los Angeles Times*, May 31, 1988, https://www.latimes.com/archives/la-xpm-1988-05-31-mn-3526-story.html.

6 Ibid.

7 Kyle Clark, "Governor Polis' Office Pressured Journalists to Delete Unfavorable Story," 9News.com, September 26, 2019, https://www.9news.com/article/news/local/next/governor-polis-office-pressured-journalists-to-delete-unfavorable-story/73-b025c3b4-db74-4875-8e13-be5294396fd0.

8 Ibid.

9 John Roberts, Quoted in E. Zimmermann, "New GOP Argument against Kagan: She Could Ban Books," *The Hill*, May 16, 2010, https://thehill.com/blogs/blog-briefing-room/news/98067-new-gop-argument-against-kagan-she-could-ban-books.

10 Federal Communications Commission, "2019 Broadband Deployment Report," May 29, 2019, https://www.fcc.gov/reports-research/reports/broadband-progress-reports/2019-broadband-deployment-report.

11 The University of Chicago, Letter to Incoming Class of 2020, https://news.uchicago.edu/sites/default/files/attachments/Dear_Class_of_2020_Students.pdf.

12 James Madison, Speech in the House of Representatives, "Annals of Congress," House of Representatives, 1st Congress, 1st Session, June 8, 1789 (Washington, DC: Gales and Seaton, 1834), p. 451-53.

13 James Madison, Anonymous Opinion Editorial, *National Gazette*, December 19, 1971.

14 Thomas Jefferson, Letter to Marquis de Lafayette, November 4, 1823.

15 Thomas Jefferson, Letter to Edward Carrington, January 16, 1787.

16 Thomas Jefferson, Letter to John Norvelle, June 11, 1807.

17 Barbara B. Oberg, ed., *The Papers of Thomas Jefferson*, vol. 30, 1 January 1798–31 January 1799 (Princeton: Princeton University Press, 2003), 550–556.

18 Jill Lepore, "Party Time," *The New Yorker*, September 10, 2007, https://www.newyorker.com/magazine/2007/09/17/party-time.

19 Woodrow Wilson Letter to House Judiciary Committee, March 22, 1917, Michael Barone, "The Law O's Using Against the Press," *New York Post*, May 28, 2013, https://nypost.com/2013/05/28/the-law-os-using-against-the-press/.

20 Abrams v. United States, 250 U.S. 616 (1919).

21 Ibid.

22 Brian Stelter, "Fox's Volley with Obama Intensifying," *The New York Times*, October 11, 2009. https://www.nytimes.com/2009/10/12/business/media/12fox.html.

23 Clarke, John Hessin, and Supreme Court Of The United States, "U.S. Reports: Abrams v. United States, 250 U.S. 616, 1919," https://www.loc.gov/item/usrep250616/.

CHAPTER 8

1 Robert J. Taylor, ed., *The Adams Papers*, vol. 1, September 1755–October 1773 (Cambridge, MA: Harvard University Press, 1977), 123–128.

2 Thomas Jefferson, "A Bill for Establishing Religious Freedom," June 12, 1779, Philip B. Kurland and Ralph Lerner, eds., *The Founders' Constitution*, Vol. 5, Amendment I, Document 37 (Chicago: The University of Chicago Press, 1986), 77.

3 Thomas Jefferson, "Replies to Public Addresses," January 1, 1802, in A.A. Lipscomb and A.E. Bergh, eds., *The Writings of Thomas Jefferson*, Vol. 16 (Washington, D.C.: Thomas Jefferson Memorial Association, 1907), 281-82.

4 Ibid.

5 Reynolds v. United States 98 U.S. 145 (1879).

6 Abraham Lincoln, "Proclamation Appointing a National Fast Day," Washington, D.C., March 30, 1863.

7 "Win at U.S. Supreme Court Leads to State-Level Challenges," Little Sisters of the Poor, http://thelittlesistersofthepoor.com/#solution.

8 Nicole Russell, "This Court Ruling Shows Why States Can't Control Artistic Expression," *Daily Signal*, September 10, 2019, https://www.dailysignal.com/2019/09/10/this -court-ruling-shows-why-states-cant-control-artistic-expression/.

9 Jennifer Latson, "What Margaret Sanger Really Said about Eugenics and Race," *Time*, October 14, 2016, https://time.com/4081760/margaret-sanger-history-eugenics/.

10 Nikki Schwab, "Candace Owens Defends Stance on White Nationalism after Contentious Hearing," *New York Post*, April 9, 2019.

11 Alexis de Tocqueville in Norman A. Graebner, "Christianity and Democracy: Tocqueville's Views of Religion in America," *The Journal of Religion*, 56, no. 3 (Jul. 1976): 263-273.

12 Martin Luther King, Jr., Sermon "A Knock at Midnight," June 5, 1963.

CHAPTER 9

1 Joseph Story, Commentaries on the Constitution of the United States, 3 vols. (Boston, 1833), in Philip B. Kurland and Ralph Lerner, eds., *The Founders' Constitution*, Vol. 5, Amendment II, Document 10 (Chicago: The University of Chicago Press, 1986), 214.

2 John Daniel Davidson, "NPR Reporter Has No Idea What 'Come and Take It' Means," *The Federalist*, October 3, 2016, https://thefederalist.com/2016/10/03/come-and-take-it/.

3 Perry Stein and Peter Hermann, "Congressman Proudly Packs a Patriotic AR-15 in His Capitol Hill Office," *The Washington Post*, April 21, 2015, https://nypost.com/2019/04/ 09/candace-owens-defends-stance-on-white-nationalism-after-contentious-hearing/, https://www.washingtonpost.com/news/local/wp/2015/04/21/congressman-proudly -packs-a-patriotic-ar-15-in-his-capitol-hill-office/.

4 Mark Gius, "An Examination of the Effects of Concealed Weapons Laws and Assault Weapons Bans on State-Level Murder Rates," *Applied Economics Letters*, Vol. 21, No. 4 (2014), 265-267.

5   John Stossel, "Myths about Gun Control," *Real Clear Politics*, October 19, 2005, https://www.realclearpolitics.com/Commentary/com-10_19_05_JS.html.

6   Firearms Control Regulations Act of 1975, District of Columbia.

7   District of Columbia v. Heller 554 U.S. 570 (2008).

8   David Kopel, "Polls: Anti-Gun Propaganda," NRA-ILA, September 13, 2000, https://www.nraila.org/articles/20000913/polls-anti-gun-propaganda-by-david-ko.

9   *The Writings of Samuel Adams 1764–1769*, Vol. I, Harry Alonzo Cushing, ed. (New York: G.P. Putnam's Sons, New York, 1904), 299.

10 William Blackstone, *Blackstone's Commentaries on the Laws of England*, Book 1, 140.

11 Richard Henry Lee, *The Pennsylvania Gazette*, February 20, 1788, Letters from the Federal Farmer to the Republican, Richard Henry Lee and Walter Bennett, eds. (Birmingham: The University of Alabama Press: 1975), 21.

12 James Madison, Speech, House of Representatives, June 8, 1789, in *The Congressional Register*, I, 423–37 (also reported in Gazette of the U.S., June 10, 1789.

13 Debates and other Proceedings of the Convention of Virginia, David Robertson, compiler (Richmond: Enquirer Press, 1805), 271.

14 To John Adams from W.H. Sumner, 3 May 1823," *Founders Online*, National Archives, https://founders.archives.gov/documents/Adams/99-02-02-7811.

15 Ibid.

16 Avianne Tan, "Man Recounts Moment He Killed Alleged Assailant of Arizona Trooper," ABC News, January 24, 2017, https://abcnews.go.com/US/man-recounts-moment-killed-assailant-allegedly-attacked-arizona/story?id=45022317.

17 Ibid.

CHAPTER 10

1   Ronald Reagan, "First Inaugural Address," January 20, 1981, in John Gabriel Hunt, ed., *The Inaugural Addresses of the Presidents* (New York: Gramercy, 1995), 471–78.

2   Ibid.

3   Ibid.

4   18 James Madison, "Federalist No. 47," *The Federalist Papers*, ed. Clinton Rossiter (New York: New American Library, 1961), 269.

5   Rachael Revesz, "Jill Stein Demands Vote Recount after Reports of Potential Hacking and Manipulation in Several Swing States," *Independent*, November 23, 2016, https://www.independent.co.uk/news/world/americas/jill-stein-green-party-election-2016-swing-state-recount-audit-votes-swing-states-scientists-hackers-a7435231.html.

6   Chuck Todd, Sally Bronston, and Matt Rivera, "Rep. John Lewis: 'I Don't See Trump As a Legitimate President,'" NBC News, January 13, 2017, https://www.nbcnews.com/storyline/meet-the-press-70-years/john-lewis-trump-won-t-be-legitimate-president-n706676.

7   Nicole Bitette, "Madonna to Crowd at Women's March: 'I've Thought a Lot about Blowing up White House,'" *New York Daily News*, January 21, 2017, https://www.nydailynews.com/entertainment/music/madonna-blowing-white-house-article-1.2952443.

8   Amy B. Wang, "Robert De Niro Goes off on Donald Trump: 'I'd like to Punch Him in the Face,'" *The Washington Post*, October 8, 2016, https://www.washingtonpost.com/news/arts-and-entertainment/wp/2016/10/08/robert-de-niro-goes-off-on-donald-trump-id-like-to-punch-him-in-the-face/.

9   "White House Statement on Acting Attorney General," CNN, January 31, 2017, https://www.cnn.com/2017/01/30/politics/white-house-statement-attorney-general/index.html.

10 Peter Baker, Lara Jakes, Julian E. Barnes, Sharon LaFraniere, and Edward Wong, "Trump's War on the 'Deep State,'" *The New York Times*, October 23, 2019, https://www.nytimes.com/2019/10/23/us/politics/trump-deep-state-impeachment.html.

11 Ibid.

12 Eric Garcia, "Bipartisan Bill Seeks to End Political 'Burrowing,'" *Roll Call*, March 7, 2018, https://www.rollcall.com/2018/03/07/bipartisan-bill-seeks-to-end-political-burrowing/.

13 Josh Gerstein and Kyle Cheney, "Comey Blasts White House for 'Lies, Plain and Simple,'" *Politico*, June 8, 2017, https://www.politico.com/story/2017/06/08/james-comey-trump-russia-testimony-239294.

14 Matea Gold, "The Campaign to Impeach President Trump Has Begun," *The Washington Post*, January 20, 2017, https://www.washingtonpost.com/news/post-politics/wp/2017/01/20/the-campaign-to-impeach-president-trump-has-begun/.

15 Ibid.

16 Rebecca Savransky, "Maxine Waters: GOP Must Confront That Trump Is 'Unstable,'" *The Hill*, October 14, 2017, https://thehill.com/homenews/house/355468-maxine-waters-gop-must-confront-that-trump-is-unstable.

17 Jason Le Miere, "Trump Impeachment Process Begins As Democrat States President 'Failed Test of Moral Leadership,'" *Newsweek*, August 17, 2017, https://www.newsweek.com/trump-impeachment-process-charlottesville-president-651925.

18 Emily Tillett, "Rep. Steve Cohen Introduces Articles of Impeachment against Trump," CBS News, November 15, 2017, https://www.cbsnews.com/news/rep-steve-cohen-introduces-new-articles-of-impeachment-against-trump/.

19 Douglas Ernst, "HuffPo Scrubs 'Ultimate Punishment' Trump Piece after Scalise, GOP Shooting," *The Washington Times*, June 15, 2017, https://www.washingtontimes.com/news/2017/jun/15/huffpo-scrubs-jason-fullers-ultimate-punishment-tr/.

20 John Wildermuth, "Rep. Jackie Speier Demands Trump's Ouster under the 25th Amendment," *San Francisco Chronicle*, August 24, 2017, https://www.sfchronicle.com/politics/article/Rep-Jackie-Speier-demands-Trump-s-ouster-under-11957020.php.

21 Gabe Sherman, "'I hate Everyone in the White House!' Trump Seethes As Advisers Fear the President Is Unraveling," *Vanity Fair*, October 11, 2017.

22 Ibid.

23 "Ajit Pai's Personal Hell, Our National Media's Failure," *Investor's Business Daily*, January 9, 2018.

24 Nicole Gallucci, "Protesters Blast Audio of Crying Children Outside Kirstjen Nielsen's House," *Mashable*, June 22, 2018, https://mashable.com/article/protestors-kirstjen-nielsen-house-crying-audio/.

25 Tim Haines, "Maxine Waters Warns Trump Cabinet: 'The People Are Going to Turn' on You," *Real Clear Politics*, June 24, 2018, https://www.realclearpolitics.com/video/2018/06/24/maxine_waters_the_people_are_going_to_turn_on_trump_enablers.html.

26 Caitlin Oprysko, "Joaquin Castro Doubles Down Amid Backlash over Tweeting Names of Trump Donors," *Politico*, August 6, 2019, https://www.politico.com/story/2019/08/06/joaquin-castro-trump-donors-1450672.

27 Ian Hanchett, "Crenshaw on Castro Donor Tweet: 'There's Another Term for This' 'It's Called Fascism'—Censure Should Be Considered," Breitbart, August 8, 2019, https://www.breitbart.com/clips/2019/08/08/crenshaw-on-castro-donor-tweet-theres-another-term-for-this-its-called-fascism-censure-should-be-considered/.

28 James Madison, Notes from Federal Convention, July 20, 1787, https://avalon.law.yale.edu/18th_century/debates_720.asp.

CHAPTER 11

1 Thomas Jefferson, Letter to Thomas McKean, July 24, 1801, https://founders.archives.gov/documents/Jefferson/01-34-02-0477.

2 Woodrow Wilson, "To Naturalized Citizens," Speech, Convention Hall, Philadelphia, Pennsylvania, May 10, 1915.

3 Martin L. King, "I Have a Dream," Speech, the March on Washington for Jobs and Freedom," Washington, D.C., August 28, 1963, http://avalon.law.yale.edu/20th_century/mlk01.asp.

4 Saul Alinsky, *Rules for Radicals* (New York: Vintage Books, 1989), 133.

5 Ibid.

6 Saul Alinsky, Interview, *Playboy Magazine*, March 1972.

7 Barack Obama, Campaign Speech, Columbia, Missouri, October 2008.

8 Janaki Chadhi, "Lynch Elementary Schools Will Lose the 'Lynch' Due to Racial Implications," *The Oregonian,* July 21, 2017, https://www.oregonlive.com/education/2017/07/lynch_elementary_schools_will.html.

9 "Our Politics Now Stupidly Trivializes Tragedy," *The Daytona Beach News-Journal,* July 13, 2018, https://www.news-journalonline.com/article/LK/20180713/OPINION/180718891/DN.

10 Ibid.

11 Paul Bedard, "Donny Deutsch: 'I'm not saying Donald Trump is going to slaughter 6 million Jews,'" *The Washington Examiner,* July 29, 2019, https://www.washingtonexaminer.com/washington-secrets/donny-deutsch-im-not-saying-trump-is-going-to-slaughter-6-million-jews.

12 National Socialist Party v. Skokie, 432 U.S. 43 (1977).

13 Calvin Sims, "The Politics of Dealing with the Threat of Boycott," *The New York Times,* March 14, 1993.

14 Veronica Stracqualursi, "New House Democrat Rashida Tlaib: 'We're Gonna Impeach the Motherf****r,'" CNN, January 4, 2019, https://www.cnn.com/2019/01/04/politics/rashida-tlaib-trump-impeachment-comments/index.html.

15 Hannah Arendt, *The Origins of Totalitarianism,* (San Diego: Harcourt, Inc, 1976): 158–184.

16 Ted Cruz, Press Release "Sen. Cruz: Open an Investigation Into Antifa, a Left-Wing Anarchist Terrorist Organization," July 23, 2019, https://www.cruz.senate.gov/?p=press_release&id=4603.

17 Reagan, "First Inaugural Address."

18 Ibid.

CHAPTER 12

1 Alexis de Tocqueville, *Democracy in America,* (New York: Bantam Dell, 2004), 665.

2   Barack Obama, "Second Inaugural Address," Washington, D.C., January 21, 2013, https://thehill.com/homenews/news/278301-text-president-obamas-second-inaugural-address.

3   Franklin D. Roosevelt, "Economic Bill of Rights," Speech, Annual Message to Congress, Washington, D.C., January 11, 1944.

4   Ibid.

5   Frank Goodnow, "The American Conception of Liberty," Speech, Providence, Rhode Island, Brown University, 1916, *The U.S. Constitution: A Reader,* ed. The Hillsdale College Politics Faculty (Hillsdale, MI: Hillsdale College Press, 2012), 631.

6   Ibid., 633.

7   George Washington, First Annual Message to a Joint Session of Congress, Federal Hall, New York City, January 8, 1790.

8   Frank S. Meyer, *In Defense of Freedom and Related Essays* (Indianapolis: Liberty Fund, Inc., 1996), 52.

9   Ibid.

10 Alexander Hamilton, "Federalist No. 69," *The Federalist Papers*, ed. Clinton Rossiter (New York: New American Library, 1961), 383-391.

11 Alexis de Tocqueville, *Democracy in America,* (New York: Bantam Dell, 2004), 665.

12 Alexis de Tocqueville, *Democracy in America,* (New York: Bantam Dell, 2004), 665.

13 John Adams to Thomas Jefferson, July 15, 1813, Postscript from Abigail Adams to Thomas Jefferson, [ca. 15 July 1813], *The Papers of Thomas Jefferson*, Retirement Series, vol. 6, *11 March to 27 November 1813*, ed. J. Jefferson Looney (Princeton: Princeton University Press, 2009), 296–298.

14 Abraham Lincoln, "Proclamation of Thanksgiving," Washington, D.C., October 3, 1863, http://www.abrahamlincolnonline.org/lincoln/speeches/thanks.htm.

CONCLUSION

1   Alexis de Tocqueville, "Discours prononcé à l'assemblée constiutante le 12 septembre 1848 sur la question du droit au travail," *Ouvres completes d'Alexis de Tocqueville* (1866), IX, 546.

2   James Madison, "The Jay Treaty," April 6, 1796, *The Founders' Constitution*: Volume 4, Article 2, Section 2, Clauses 2 and 3, Document 22 (Chicago: The University of Chicago Press, 1987), 81–85.

3   Russell Kirk, *Prospects for Conservatives* (Chicago: Henry Regnery Company, 1956), 264.

4   Edmund Burke, *Reflections on the French Revolution & Other Essays* by Edmund Burke (New York: Everyman's Library, 2015), https://archive.org/stream/reflectionsonthe005907mbp/reflectionsonthe005907mbp_djvu.txt.

5   Daniel Webster, Speech, Delivered before the New York Historical Society, February 23, 1852, (New York: Press of the Historical Society, 1852), https://archive.org/stream/addressdelivered00webs/addressdelivered00webs_djvu.txt.

6   Ibid.

7   F.A. Hayek, *The Road to Serfdom*, (Chicago: The University of Chicago Press, 1994), 30-31.

8   Alexis de Tocqueville, "Discours prononcé à l'assemblée constiutante le 12 septembre 1848 sur la question du droit au travail," *Ouvres completes d'Alexis de Tocqueville* (1866), IX, 546.

9 Franklin D. Roosevelt, "Annual Message to Congress," Washington, DC, January 6, 1941, https://www.fdrlibrary.org/four-freedoms.

10 Michael Howard Saul, "Bloomberg Loses in Sugary Drinks Fight," *The Wall Street Journal,* July 30, 2013, https://www.wsj.com/articles/SB1000142412788732435470457 8638223419343406.

Acknowledgments

I am sincerely thankful to my good friends for their advice, encouragement, fact-checking, and insights. Mike Lee, Jim DeMint, Ed Corrigan, Ritika Robertson, James Hampson, Chris Jaarda, and James Wallner each provided invaluable support throughout the writing of this book. David Barton and Tim Barton helped ignite my interest in the Capitol's history, and have been steadfast friends over the years. Thanks to each of you for your contagious love for our nation's history.

This book could not have been completed without the assistance of Andrew Dentemaro in the office of the Architect of the Capitol and Matthew Wasniewski, historian for the U.S. House of Representatives.

Finally, to my family, Perry, Cody and Lindsey, Kaitlin and Matt, Bear, Bo, and Sugar Ray: my deepest gratitude. Your constant encouragement and love throughout my career, but especially during the writing of this book, made it possible for me to pursue this project. Words can never express how grateful I am.